Fiona is a retired Registered Nurse who enjoyed a nursing career spanning both the public sector and private sectors in Australia, with the majority in the acute private sector. With her background as one of the last hospital-trained Registered Nurses in Australia, her extensive years as an operating theatre nurse and Perioperative Services Manager, as well as her climb to Nursing Executive Leadership roles including Director of Clinical Services and Director of Nursing roles, her memoir *Third Time's a Charm* details the challenges of traversing executive leadership in the Australian private healthcare sector.

She demonstrates that it can be a fantastic career, but like anything, can have its challenges and pitfalls – her tips are definitely worth noting for an easier climb up that career ladder.

Fiona is also an ovarian cancer survivor, one of the few diagnosed at stage 2 who is still here to tell the tale about her dance with the she-devil ovarian cancer. Her story details her diagnosis in 2015, her recurrence in 2020 and how she has been surviving as a chronic ovarian cancer sufferer ever since. She hopes to demonstrate with her story that just because you are diagnosed with cancer it does not mean it is the end of the world and that you can in fact continue to work, thrive and get on with living in spite of it.

I would like to dedicate my memoir, *Third time's a charm*, to my partner and love in life, Phillip. We were high school sweethearts, got married young and proceeded to grow up together. You have had my back through all the trials and tribulations of my career, when other people possibly should have. I thank you for not punching out a couple of the blokes you really wanted to and for helping me keep my shitty necessary career secrets, while always helping me to believe I could do and be anything. Your ongoing strength as we fight my cancer battle has been and remains amazing and has helped me always know that I will do whatever I need to do for survival, even when it sometimes sucks! Love you always!

Fiona Brown

THIRD TIME'S A CHARM

AUSTIN MACAULEY PUBLISHERS
LONDON · CAMBRIDGE · NEW YORK · SHARJAH

Copyright © Fiona Brown 2025

The right of Fiona Brown to be identified as author of this work has been asserted by the author in accordance with sections 77 and 78 of the Copyright, Designs and Patents Act 1988.

All rights reserved. No part of this publication may be reproduced, stored in a retrieval system, or transmitted in any form or by any means, electronic, mechanical, photocopying, recording, or otherwise, without the prior permission of the publishers.

Any person who commits any unauthorised act in relation to this publication may be liable to criminal prosecution and civil claims for damages.

All of the events in this memoir are true to the best of author's memory. The views expressed in this memoir are solely those of the author.

A CIP catalogue record for this title is available from the British Library.

ISBN 9781035879670 (Paperback)
ISBN 9781035879687 (ePub e-book)

www.austinmacauley.com

First Published 2025
Austin Macauley Publishers Ltd®
1 Canada Square
Canary Wharf
London
E14 5AA

I would like to acknowledge the fantastic team at Austen Macauley Publishers for your help and support bringing my story into the world. I would also like to give special acknowledgement to my team of Medical Oncologists, from my initial one in Toowoomba who helped me through the terror of an ovarian cancer diagnosis, my Wesley Oncologist who managed my initial recurrence and finally my brilliant current Oncologist A/Prof Jermaine (Jim) Coward - Thank you to you all for getting me to where I am today!

Acknowledgement of some of the great female leaders/mentors I experienced and had the luck to learn from should go to Jo Standen (Perioperative Services Super Consultant), Jenny Duncan (DCS Extraordinaire) and Kim Chant (My first taste of a fabulous acting female CEO). Thank you ladies – you rock!

And last but far from least is my acknowledgement and gratitude to my Mum, Joan Chapman, who set me on a road to survival all those years ago with her phone call about her ovarian cancer – Thanks Mum.

Once upon a time in a land far away—well, actually not really that far, just a little way over the Queensland/New South Wales border in Grafton on the NSW north coast—lived a little girl who grew up not knowing what she wanted to be. She tried being an admin person with Australia Post in Sydney for three months, which was a mega fail, and then she decided to try being a nurse—and that little girl was me, you can call me Princess Fiona! Nah, just kidding!

I am pretty sure I was not the only wannabe princess who had no clue what their life calling would be, and I remain ecstatic that I managed to fall into mine all those years ago. I got to have an awesome career as a nurse for the 40 odd years I got to work, with the latter 25 years as a senior manager in the private sector.

Was every year and every job awesome? Yeah, nah! I had my great experiences and my shitty experiences, much like everybody does, I imagine, and I definitely never envisioned that I would post-note my career with a tell-all tale about some of those experiences, but there you go.

I have read a few tell-all books about the healthcare sector, including the horror Bundaberg debacle with Dr Patel, but I have never read anything about the games we, or rather, mainly the big boss boys, play in senior hospital management in the private sector in Australia.

The boys at the top and sadly, in many cases, it is still the 'boys', pretty much ensure that no-one ever says anything about some of our shitty experiences because we are all so desperate to get that next job and have that much-needed reference—that we toe the line like the good little princesses or rather nurses that we are. But bad luck, boys, I am fat out of caring and well and truly retired and out of your reach.

Why do I think my fairy-tale is worth telling? You are right, I am no-one too special, just another Registered Nurse with a story and I am aware that our healthcare system is full of us.

But part of what drives me is to demonstrate to everyone, not just nurses, that just because you get a cancer diagnosis, it's not the end of the world for you. Yes, I got a really shitty one in December 2015, but I am still here to tell the tale!

Life goes on, some for longer than others, and you just have to accept it and keep living through it. I also don't know where I'm going when I leave this world, but choose to believe it is going to be to somewhere amazing.

No, I am not religious but trust me that when you get close to looking the big guy in the eye, you might adapt your beliefs a little to make what's coming a little less scary. The other reality is that in order to know where you are going, you need to know where you have been and when I do leave this world, I would like my loved ones, friends and old colleagues to know where I have really been.

I would expect the majority of people I mention by job title to be long retired and if they are not, then quite frankly, they should probably think about it. Just saying. If you ever knew me and are up for the challenge, good luck trying to figure out who was who in my zoo. I'll never tell!

First up, I would like to sincerely apologise to all the people I have told a fairy story to, about my career background at some stage during my time working with you. It always killed me that I had to maintain the lie to maintain my career.

The reality was that I was the main breadwinner, and I needed that next job and if telling a furfy about why I may have left somewhere was how I could do it, then do it I would.

What my career has taught me is that you should never judge those people that you hear are suddenly out of a job—the truth of what has happened is usually much more twisted than what you hear, and the person involved has probably been gagged and is unable to spell out what really happened.

So, give them your understanding and grace; there is a fair chance they deserve both. Life lesson one for having a long management career in the private healthcare sector—if you want to survive long without mishap, your best bet is to shut up and not rock the boat.

Do not pop your head up where men with power will see you—do not be a right fighter! As my story unfolds, it will eventually become apparent that I did not follow my own advice. What can I say? Hindsight is a beautiful thing.

I learnt a number of lessons during my 40-year career, particularly the latter 22 years as a perioperative services manager and director of clinical services/director of nursing—and one of the most important was that you cannot hide what you are.

What I mean by this is that much like a leopard cannot change its spots, we poor old humans cannot really successfully pretend to be something we are not for any extended period of time. So essentially, if you are a crap nurse or manager or whatever, this will become clear to others sooner or later—good luck hiding it for the 6 months probationary period currently allowed by Fair Work Australia. Alternatively, if you are a star, this soon becomes apparent too—if the right people are looking.

Throughout my tale, I will also touch on some of the other lessons I would encourage any new nurse manager to take note of, whether in the private sector or the public—I am sure many of them are relevant to both healthcare sectors.

With the gift of hindsight and the fact that I am the one steering this trip down memory lane, I have decided to include what I wished I had been able to say at the time of some of my experiences—my chance to finally have the last say that I could never have at the time.

I have also included some of the lessons I learnt from each role and what I could have done better—regularly taking a moment of insight to review your own performance is something that may well save you a lot of grief further down the track.

I am hoping that some young aspiring Registered Nurse leader will read my story and learn from it. That my experience will help them to traverse the minefield of being a nurse leader in the private sector in Australia.

Any errors in recollections are mine alone—sorry—age, menopause and chemo brain truly are things. Or as the late Queen Elizabeth II put it so succinctly, "Recollections may vary," and these are mine.

I grew up in Grafton in northern NSW, one of the straggling end of the baby boomers group born in 1962. My years growing up were pretty great, filled with not being particularly fabulous at school, but being a bit better at sport including sprint running and hockey.

My weekends were a fabulous mix of fishing at multiple beachside spots including Iluka, Wooli and Browns Rocks—my father was a keen fisherman and if I would have preferred, we would have gone to a popular beach like Yamba; in hindsight, I know how lucky I was to get to go fishing anywhere.

Growing up in Grafton, the jacaranda capital of Australia, was pretty fabulous too where we had the freedom to ride our bikes to and from school and there did not seem to be any of the risks to children that there are today.

Yeah, I know, more likely, the monsters were better at hiding back then. I am one of the lucky ones who had none of that ugliness in my life who can profess that I have only good memories growing up.

My first adventure was as a postal clerk with Australia Post—not a career I was pining for but one that would give me an income. I had been forced to do an admin type course at Grafton TAFE after finishing high school and being on the dole, as we called unemployment benefits back then.

I finished school with no clue about what I wanted to be when I grew up. The fact that I had to move to Sydney and live with a distant cousin on my father's side and her family that I had never met before, initially seemed to be a part of the adventure.

I managed to last 3 months in the big smoke where I made a few new friends and caught up with some old school friends before returning to Grafton for Christmas and then deciding that I would only go back to Sydney to quit—my little country girl heart was not loving my life in Sydney.

It was catching up with old school friends after my hasty return to Grafton who had gone directly into nursing after school that sparked the idea that I might be a nurse. I think I had always thought that I needed to be a lot smarter than I felt I was to get into general nurse training—what a fabulous surprise it was to realise that I actually wasn't too stupid.

So, life lesson, peeps—never sell yourself short and if you want to do something—go for it. What is the worst thing that can happen? You don't get to do what you wanted. But unless you try, you will never know if you could have succeeded at it or not.

I sent off my application to start the three-year general nurse training course on offer at Grafton Base Hospital and was then lucky enough to start my nursing career in one of the last hospital-based general nurse training programs at Grafton Base Hospital in 1981.

I still lived at home throughout the first couple of years of my training since my childhood home was literally a 5-minute walk around the corner. And back in those days, there was no fear walking home late at night as a lone female.

I would have been more worried about being chased by a dog than an actual person. It was during these early days of nursing that my hubby and I rekindled our high school relationship, the beginnings of our now 38+ years marriage and longer relationship—he deserves full credit for being along on this career ride with me, often being the only person other than me who knew what was really going on.

Grafton Base Hospital was not a very big hospital but in hindsight, it was punching above its weight with the nurse training it offered its staff. We started our general nurse training with 12 weeks in the on-site training centre for probationary training school or PTS as it was known.

Those initial 12 weeks were a fabulous time of spending our days in the school and doing supervised visits to the wards. We learnt how to take blood pressures on the old pump-up blood pressure machines and how to give intramuscular needles using oranges.

A scary thought, but this process probably still works in university simulated training rooms to this day, although I am not sure any baby nurses these days could use a non-electronic blood pressure machine.

We would complete placements in different specialty areas of the hospital, rotating through most ward areas during the three years of our training. I remember starting my first clinical rotation in the medical ward and being absolutely terrified sitting through patient handover with night staff and knowing I had eight patients to look after when I really kind of felt I had no freaking idea what I was doing.

I was lucky with that very first rotation that I scored 'Sheila', my diabetic, loud, possible personality disorder patient now that I think about it, as one of my first patients. I would credit her for actually giving me the basics of how to plan my day.

She wore a wig that she would style every day and a full face of over-the-top makeup and was a regular patient to the ward, so knew its routine really well. Grafton Base used patient allocation as a nursing model of care, which generally meant that we each received two four-bed wards totalling eight patients each, or when we were more experienced, the six single rooms with sicker patients.

We were expected to do everything for those eight patients from showering them or giving them a sponge bath, all of their drug administration and any other cares such as dressings during our eight-hour shift.

We did not have any good fairy assistant in nursing to come along and do the showers for us and only occasionally, if we had a very heavy patient, would our patient be showered by the wards man, or we would be assisted by the wards man to do it ourselves.

So, on my first day, I was more than a bit frazzled after sitting through our morning patient care handover from night duty staff and trying to decide what I needed to do first. As a consequence of my dithering, I was late with Sheila's insulin, which she needed to have before her breakfast.

I think I only got it to her when I did because she buzzed me to find out where it was. After a rushed morning where I finally managed to draw breath, Sheila again buzzed me and offered me a solution.

She explained that she knew the running of the ward very well due to her being a long-term patient and asked would I be offended if she buzzed me to remind me what needed doing when.

I thought she was a godsend and told her I would love her help getting me organised—who knows how many of us baby nurses she deserved the credit for training—more than just me I would wager. Thankfully, I only needed her guidance for a few days before I got the hang of planning out my day.

Basically, starting with any early medications required before or with breakfast, setting patients up in showers or actually taking them out and helping them throughout the process, rushing out to make their bed while they are ideally managing for a few minutes on their own.

I could credit one of my fellow male nursing students for giving me a crash course in how to give a gentleman a shave since this was also a requirement, particularly with some of our older gents who wanted a shave every day to feel spic and span.

Women do not naturally know how to get a good lather up or how to get a man to move his face and chin to allow you to do the best job. We ideally managed to get everyone all cleaned up and in nice clean sheets by morning teatime that usually came about 10, which was also the time that a lot of patients had drugs to be given.

Then, we would have time between morning tea and lunch to complete any dressings, etc. that needed doing as well as ensure any midday medications were available. Sometimes, one of our patients may have needed assistance with feeding, so we would do that too.

Again, there was no assistant in nursing to help us—we all had to do what needed doing for each of our patients. After lunch, we would have our report to write up on each patient as well as 2pm medications to administer.

It is worth noting that during all of this, we were answering any buzzers for toileting assistance or pain complaints or whatever a patient may summon us for. Needless to say, we felt like we had worked a good hard day by the time we finished.

The good news was that at least at that time, the doctors would normally do their rounds with the ward nurse unit manager and we only had to accompany them if she or he was tied up.

Many healthcare organisations have fostered a team-work nursing model of care for decades, which was kind of what used to be in place way back before my time where the student nurses did all the crap jobs and the staff nurses (or Registered Nurse) swanned around and did the medications and the dressings.

In later years, this has helped address a shortage of Registered Nurses and a surplus of assistant nurses, which are often undergraduate Registered Nurses currently undertaking their university degree since nursing training has now been in universities for years.

I have been asked many times whether I believe hospital-based training or university training was best and I can only answer that based on my own experience and my years of exposure in leadership roles—yes, I do think hospital-based training was better.

Why? Because after that initial 12 weeks of PTS, we spent more time in the wards working as a student nurse with our own patients with only short stints in the training school. Any of my classmates who discovered early on that cleaning up shitty bums or whatever other unpleasant task awaited us could determine easily whether this was what they really wanted to do and pull out there and then.

Current student nurses do not really get exposed to what being a nurse is really like until they finish their three-year university degree and commence (hopefully) a graduate nurse program, where they actually have to be taught how to really be a nurse and actually have full responsibility for a number of patients.

A lesson they are only getting when they are supposed to already be a Registered Nurse, whereas once we completed our three years hospital-based training and passed our general nursing examination, we were a Registered Nurse and were good to go—we did not need another twelve months to teach us how to be a fulltime nurse.

This debate could go on for years with many arguing that nursing had to move to tertiary institutions to give the career the respect it needed. Alternatively, we can surmise that we followed what they did in the United States and interestingly, there has been talk in recent years of the benefits of moving back to a hospital-based more patient-care intense training experience.

So, if they swap back, no doubt we in Australia will too and suggest that it was our idea all along. The other undeniable benefit of hospital-based training was that we were earning a wage immediately and the hospital always had ample staff because they would have a new intake every year.

There was never a shortage of applicants because it was a great job opportunity with an instant income. If nothing else, I believe the latter would ensure that any nurse shortages looming on our horizons would be minimised.

Of course, having one 3-hour exam to evaluate three years of work as occurred in the past is a big no and this could be addressed with regular course work, assignments and exams throughout the three-year on-site training program.

Any hospital offering an on-site training program would also need an appropriate training area with suitable educators employed full time.

I acknowledge that my training was a long, long time ago and current nurses, no matter how they are trained, are unlikely to replicate some of my experiences.

There was a lovely lady I cared for with Guillain-Barre syndrome where she could walk but could not use her arms, so I had to assist her with all of her meals and other activities of daily living.

I also had the job of helping her have a cigarette. This, if nothing else, shows you just how very long ago this was because patients at that time (1981-1982ish) were allowed to smoke in hospital.

I would light up her cigarette for her while she sat on her chair in the four-bed ward and then hold it for her for subsequent inhalations. I did the ash butting, etc. and it helped that at that time of my life, I too was a grotty little smoker. Just one memory that is never forgotten despite the passage of time and life in-between.

Another is of the young eighteen-month-old child that was admitted with an ear infection and another nurse and I had to syringe out her ear with peroxide and collect the writhing maggots that washed out in the process. I know—bluck—some things can never be unseen.

We did it because we had to help that little child and if we took turns at dry retching as we did it, then that was ok. We stopped and refused to continue because it was so traumatic for both the child and us and quite frankly, it would probably be deemed assault now.

These are just a couple of examples of what I got to experience and see while working at Grafton Base Hospital, though there were many more.

During what I think was my third year of general nurse training, the big decision was made by the public health nurse power brokers that nurses in NSW no longer had to wear the student nursing caps that we had worn since commencing.

After the number of times we females had managed to hook our nursing cap ensconced heads on equipment at one time or another, it was with great joy that we celebrated by tossing them in the air for a photo-op with our local newspaper.

We had worn a light blue button-down dress with brown shoes (and nursing cap) and once we graduated and became Registered Nurses, we progressed to a white button-down dress with white shoes.

This was where the description that someone had 'white shoe syndrome' came from, which was generally used to describe a newly qualified Registered Nurse who became carried away with how important they were and how much they could boss student nurses around. Not necessarily a title to try to aspire to!

At the completion of our three-year general nurse training, those of us at Grafton Base Hospital had to travel over to Lismore to sit our general nurse examination. It was a massive exam, which basically supposedly measured all of our three years of learning.

Unfortunately for me and a few of my classmates, we did not pass first time around and had to re-sit the exam some weeks later. Thankfully, we all managed to pass it the second time around and it was no surprise in later times that I blitzed anatomy related subjects both times and struggled more with the medical physiological issues.

We happily got to graduate with the remainder of our class wearing the massive white paper veils, which, thank goodness, were only worn at these graduation ceremonies by that time in Grafton.

I finished my training during the doctors' strike in 1984 and as a consequence, it took me some time to finally be employed full time back at Grafton Base Hospital.

For some months, I was casual and I made myself available for every shift I was offered—a good lesson for any casual nurses out there that are after a permanent job—it's the nurse who is always available and reliable who will be offered the contracted job.

I then spent probably the first twelve months or so rotating from ward to ward as a permanent reliever. It was around this time in September 1985 that Phillip and I married, squeezing our wedding in after the footy season finished—Phillip by this time was playing with the local footy club, Ghosts.

In what was at the time amazing luck, for some reason, the director of nursing decided to meet with all of the nursing staff and do a bit of a performance review with each of us.

I remember telling her that I was not really enjoying the acute medical ward or constantly rotating to relieve other staff—that I longed for somewhere and something to put my teeth into and that I liked the surgical ward. With the luck that has followed me throughout my career, at least some of the time, she listened.

Within a short period of time, I was moved to work in the recovery ward with the lovely Registered Nurse that ran recovery—we were a two-woman team, and it was a nice change from ward work.

I loved it and loved being a part of the close-knit little team in theatres. I was rocking along in my recovery RN role for 12 months or so, not much thinking about what I wanted to be when I grew up, let alone in ten years.

Then one afternoon, the theatre nurse unit manager and one of the clinical nurse specialists decided to change my life. They thought that it was time for me to learn to be a scrub nurse—I laughed at them both because I thought they were kidding.

When the theatre nurse unit manager said she was deadly serious, I kind of said, "Oh, ok then," and got on with learning all I could. To their credit, they made sure I was introduced smoothly to scrubbing (where you pass the instruments to the surgeon) with lots of opportunity to double scrub with the experienced Registered Nurses, this being really the best way to learn to be a scrub nurse.

You get to do everything but have the experienced Registered Nurse there to help you if things get scary or you get out of your depth. This ensures the surgeon does not get too stressed either, something always critical because after all, they are the one doing the surgery.

The clinical nurse specialist encouraged me to hit the textbooks and learn as much as I could about each surgical procedure I scrubbed for well before I scrubbed for it—a worthwhile lesson for any learning theatre nurse.

The pictures in the textbook may not look exactly like the actual anatomy during surgery but it gave you a really good idea about how the surgery would flow, making you a far better more instinctive scrub nurse able to anticipate what the surgeon needed next.

I then discovered I had found my true calling as a nurse, at least my first calling—I absolutely loved scrubbing for just about any operation I could, and it did not take long for me to hunger for more than Grafton Base Hospital could deliver in the way of operating theatre experience.

For a small two theatre operating theatre unit, I got to see our multi-talented general surgeons do everything from skin lesions to abdominal aortic aneurysms, to fractured hips and burr holes in a skull.

Grafton did not have plastic surgeons, vascular surgeons, orthopaedic or neurosurgeons at that time—our great general surgeons did a bit of everything with general and colorectal probably their real specialties—I never appreciated how amazing they were until later in my career.

In Grafton Base operating theatres, I also had the terrible experience of seeing a young man with a lacerated calf muscle from a motorbike accident deteriorate and die from malignant hyperthermia—an extremely rare complication that most theatre nurses never see in their career and thankfully, something I never saw again.

This rare complication caused by an anaesthetic agent that we used at that time needed a specific drug called Dantrolene to treat it, and unfortunately at that time in GBH, we did not have a large enough supply of it to have any great effect.

The young man's muscles overheated and we had to try to cool him with ice and then manage him in cardiac arrest. We had many staff in the theatre that night including the scrub team and the hospital arrest team, and we were all shell-shocked when we had to accept that we could not save him.

The theatre nurse unit manager tasked me with creating an emergency 'malignant hyperthermia' kit after this and it was possibly one of the most important tasks I ever completed in my nursing career.

Due to its very rarity, it's highly likely Grafton Base Hospital has never seen another case and I hope I don't somehow jinx them with this mention. I would also anticipate that every operating theatre in the country has a similar emergency malignant hyperthermia kit with sufficient Dantrolene on hand, or within easy access, to successfully treat the patient if it ever occurred.

Due to the rarity of this emergency occurring, hospitals have the issue of the drug Dantrolene expiring before it is ever needed—hospitals often agree to pool their supply with other nearby hospitals to help manage this since it is, of course, also a very expensive drug.

The drug has to be given in mg per kg, so multiple ampoules are usually needed. The good news was that the anaesthetic agent that was attributed with causing this reaction was discontinued decades ago.

During 1989, I became more and more fixated on wanting to go to a large city to increase my theatre skills and knowledge and with that in mind, I applied to do the operating theatre course at Royal North Shore Hospital, desperate to be accepted but also wary that I may be too far away in the country and not in a big enough theatre unit to have sufficient theatre experience to be considered.

The help I received from the other scrub nurses with this was amazing and I am sure, helped me to be successful with my application. My husband and I were also both a bit over Grafton and its lack of opportunity (at least I was) and I convinced him that the best thing for us to do was to head to Sydney, so I could do my theatre course, if I got in.

God love him—when I was accepted into the course, he took my hand, and we started our adventure in the big smoke together. He moved before me after getting a job with Telecom, as Telstra was known then, with the help of a mate, which was good because it helped him acclimate to Sydney a bit—I was way more excited about the move than he was.

My baby sister Janis came with us to round out our little family affair. The fabulous gang in the theatres at Grafton Base gave me a great send-off party and the pre-requisite dunking in the scrub sink and plastering of my legs together with Plaster of Paris.

Can't say that I ever had such a great send-off ever again! I can only be grateful that smart phones did not exist at that time because me jumping around with my legs plastered together would have made an amazing meme or Tik Tok video.

This latter, along with many other fantastic memories, accompanied me when I left Grafton Base. We had so much fun during our general nurse training and afterwards with parties in the nurse's quarter, or more often in the resident medical officer quarters.

If we knew anything, then the Grafton Base nurses knew how to party! I suspect our on-site training contributed to this because we all became pretty close after working together for so long.

Leaving Grafton was a positive experience as I set off on a huge career adventure, so fortunately, I did not have any conversations that I wished I had said at the time. Other than 'so long and thanks for the memories'.

My adventure in the big smoke started in late 1989, following our relocation to Sydney in early December. Since my operating theatre management certificate course did not start until the February in 1990, I still needed to do something to contribute to the rent and our lifestyle, so I joined a nursing agency where I would work night shifts in the wards.

I was too afraid to put myself forward for the operating theatre specific nursing agency ASEPS because at that stage, I was still convinced I would not be skilled enough. I figured that by working a night shift I would be with another nurse and with the patients expected to be mostly asleep, I would be able to manage their minimal care requirements.

I did shifts all over Sydney, including a few out at what was then Prince Henry Hospital out near Long Bay jail. It was there that I ended up in what was an AIDs wards at that time—something I found really shocking after Grafton Base Hospital; however, it was a timely lesson because I saw young patients who had AIDs they had contracted through a blood transfusion.

It demonstrated to me the reality of that terrible disease and how the population could be making assumptions and feeding their prejudices about it being a homosexual disease when it was, in fact, nothing of the sort.

I was really lucky to work on shift with a male nurse who really educated me about what I needed to do to protect myself and it really only came down to the basic principles I had learnt in nursing, in particular in theatres, that I needed to protect myself from all blood and body fluids.

It also brought home those lessons from Lady Di in her hospital visits that touching someone with AIDs was not going to give it to me. It stood me in good stead as I got ready to start my operating theatre course, which really drummed into us the importance of standard precautions where we needed to treat everyone the same to protect both us and them.

Back in those early days, patients rarely wanted to put their hand up and tell you they had AIDs or HIV because they were terrified of being treated differently.

I got to complete my operating theatre management course at Royal North Shore Hospital and this 12-month course, which started in February 1990, showed me how very little Grafton Base Hospital was.

It also showed me that I may have been better prepared than perhaps some of my course colleagues—we were a hodgepodge mix pulled from northern NSW and northern Sydney—apparently, little old me in Grafton fell into their catchment area, which was part of why I was successful at getting into the theatre course.

I am grateful for that to this day. I can still remember the surprise on the face of our anaesthetic lecturer during the course when I could report that I had indeed seen a malignant hyperthermia patient in little ol' Grafton.

This is also the anaesthetic lecturer who, unfortunately, had the joy of teaching us after lunch for our anaesthetic viva lectures. And we all know what happens after lunch, dead mullet syndrome or postprandial somnolence, which one of my Grafton student lecturers described as the food coma that follows eating and refers to the sense of fatigue, general sleepiness and decreased energy levels that you can get after eating a meal.

God help us if he had ever got us after Christmas lunch! He used to counter this by whacking whichever one of us was unfortunate enough to doze off with the long pointer he liked to wave about during class.

Again that would probably be deemed assault these days too. Mind you, it worked, because even if we were not the whackee receiving the prod, it made enough noise to scare the living daylights out of the rest of us.

My general nurse training at Grafton Base and my operating theatre course at Royal North Shore Hospital were all completed in the NSW public health system and throughout this time, it had never occurred to me that I might one day end up in the private health system; after all, Grafton did not even have a private hospital.

During the completion of my theatre course at Royal North Shore Hospital, I lived in Croydon Park in inner western Sydney, and we never had enough cars in the household for me to drive, so I pretty much learnt to find my way to St Leonards via the train system.

Thankfully, due to permanent night staff, we never had to work night shifts while completing the course. Grafton Base Hospital very considerately allowed me to take leave without pay for the twelve months of the theatre course with the hope that I would return and take all of that newly learnt knowledge back to them.

I knew shortly into my theatre course, and into our new life in Sydney, that I had no intention of going back to Grafton and resigned formally from them as soon as I made that decision.

Completing the theatre course at Royal North Shore was possibly the beginning of me growing that small degree of arrogance I associate with nurses in general, but theatre nurses in particular. (Oh yeah, ICU nurses—I see you too.)

We really did think we were a bit special. Not in a bad way but in a clever way. I know—the absolute arrogance of that, but the truth is that at Royal North Shore Hospital, we were made to feel like we were special.

It started with the lesson about how to tie our paper theatre hats (pink to designate we were theatre course trainees and complete plebs) to be some great peaked monstrosity and ended with us rotating through the various mega specialities in this major teaching hospital.

I got to scrub for spines and hearts and so many other things, with last but far from least, neurosurgery.

It was here that I learnt what an organ harvest was too—yep, it pretty much is exactly what it sounds like. When a patient has generously donated their organs if they die or are considered brain dead, then that patient is taken to the theatres where a specialised transplant team proceeds to remove all of the organs that have been donated, prepping them carefully to ensure the gift is not wasted before it arrives to its lucky recipient.

I got to scrub as part of the theatre team for one of these and the thing I still remember the most is the silence that enveloped the theatre when everything had been removed and the patient was finally pronounced deceased.

Between all of the instruments that go ping and make noise in an operating theatre, the absolute silence was deafening. I still get goose bumps thinking of that person, and more importantly, their family, making that sacrifice to allow someone else to live. Absolute legends!

At that time, the operating theatre course grad class had to apply to a specialty area for a job when the theatre course completed. I had long since decided to get a job closer to my home in Croydon Park if I could and had been accepted at a little private hospital in Ashfield called the Masonic.

I could walk there in 15 minutes from home, so I thought it was perfect. It had four brand new operating theatres, which I figured was enough for me at that time. I did not apply to any of the specialty areas at Royal North Shore Hospital because I had no intention of staying and it was only towards the very end of my time there that the neuro staff finally deigned to tell me that I was staying with them.

I must admit to taking no small measure of satisfaction from telling them, "No, actually, I am very sorry but I am leaving." They could not believe I would pass up such an honour—this from the scary as hell Registered Nurses who would put you in the operating theatre with 2 trolleys of neuro equipment to set up using large photo pictures on the walls as a guide.

They would then time you before coming back and judging you and only finding the one pair of forceps placed a 1/2 inch too far to the right, rather than everything else perfectly placed.

Yeah, nah! Not my cup of tea. This experience was the beginning of the shaping of me into a Registered Nurse who preferred to teach by friendly example with support rather than what could look like the bullying snobbishness I had experienced in the neurosurgical specialty at Royal North Shore Hospital. Hopefully that is no longer how things work at Royal North Shore Hospital.

This flowed through to many things at the hospital, including the specialist surgeon doctors of that time, with consultants having to be addressed as Mr to differentiate them from all of the surgical registrars and resident doctors, both still completing their training that would be part of each surgical team at the hospital at that time—I know I likely pissed off more than one bigwig because I kept calling them lowly Dr.

Some things never change though, as I would discover time and again throughout my career. A key lesson from completing my operating theatre certificate experience was that you shape yourself to your environment, you do not expect them to change shape for you—you are the implant!

It was an ongoing lesson after I left to not keep saying, "At Royal North Shore, we did it like this." No surer way to piss staff off where you now were. And you know those neurosurgery nurses were actually legends because I could probably do a trolley setup to their standards even now.

Again, leaving Royal North Shore Hospital was not a negative experience, so I did not have anything I felt I wished I had said to anyone. I only spent the 12 months of the operating theatre management course there and really had only got to know my fellow course participants well.

For my sit-down review with myself after leaving Royal North Shore Hospital, I have asked myself three questions:

1. What did I do well at Royal North Shore Hospital? Learn; that was the key thing I was there to do since I was completing my operating theatre management course. I got to rotate through every specialty in this major teaching hospital and subsequently, developed some excellent operating theatre skills that made me a valuable asset at every theatre job I had that followed. Royal North Shore Hospital was recognised as a centre of excellence and being able to include my stop there on my CV moving forward was key to many of my later achievements, I think.
2. What could I have done better? I could have given more thought to whether I should have stayed there for another 12 months to really embed by skillset; however, I was in too much of a hurry to move on and

spread my wings in the big smoke. I really did not give much thought to whether my move to the Masonic was a good career idea—I was just focused on making it easier to get to wherever I was working. In later years, I learnt to travel to wherever I needed to and that you don't move house every time you move jobs in Sydney; you just figure out how to get there.

3. What was my major take away from Royal North Shore Hospital? I learnt that if you put your head down and listen to what you are being shown and taught that you can learn to do just about anything. Our first 3 months of our theatre course were taken up doing our anaesthetic and recovery rotations and we were all hungry to get into what we were there for—learning to scrub for anything and everything. But that delay was key, and we learnt valuable skills such as how to prepare a patient for their major surgery including setting up and assisting with insertion of central lines and all the other things necessary to keep a patient alive throughout their procedure. The first time I looked over the anaesthetic screen during my anaesthetic rotation in the cardiothoracic theatre, I was in equal parts awe and absolute terror at seeing that heart sitting there beating away before it was plugged into the bypass machine, which then bypassed the patient's entire blood-flow through the bypass machine. The scrub nurses appeared to be magicians as they kept ahead of the surgical team all while suturing the leg wounds where the veins had been stripped to use during the

surgery. The fact that I was able to be that scrub nurse, with a bit of help, by the end of my theatre course, was amazing and a true testament to how well Royal North Shore Hospital had taught us during our twelve-month operating theatre management course.

By this stage, I had been a Registered Nurse for all of six years, so I was still a baby really. I had been really impressed by the director of nursing at the Masonic who had recruited me—she had taken me around the hospital and showed me the new theatre suite, which was not the least of what attracted me to this little four-theatre complex.

Being personally welcomed and shown around was also a first lesson in how a little bit of attention from a person in power can really impact your perspective as a baby employee. I was fortunate to start on Monday, the same day that all the other theatre staff moved to the new complex, so consequently, I was no more lost than anybody else.

I quickly discovered that I was the only staff member other than the theatre manager that had an operating theatre certificate and subsequently, within no time at all, it seemed I was being put as acting theatre manager whenever the real one was off.

I am not sure what happened to her but with years of hindsight, I expect she was pushed out by management at the time. They may well have thought they had a backup in me, and this did nothing but scare the crap out of this little country mouse.

Yes, I thought I was pretty special after finishing my theatre course at Royal North Shore Hospital but by no means did I think I should be running the place. At that time, I did not enjoy the responsibility of having to go to the director of nursing or chief executive officer or whoever the dude was in-charge in the big house—(yes, there literally was one right beside the hospital) to beg to be able to buy some new piece of equipment desperately needed.

I quickly determined that I preferred the apparent bottomless pit of the public sector purse where equipment was always available when you needed it. And I certainly did not have to be the one to do the asking for it.

The Masonic was my first experience in a private hospital and for the most part, working in the theatres seemed the same as working in any public hospital operating theatre suite with maybe a slight difference being how we were expected to pander to the surgeons.

The other glaring difference was the presence of a bundy clock system where every staff member had a bundy card that we had to clock on and off with—that was definitely something I had never seen before.

Of course, staff tried to work their way around it and sometimes get a colleague to bundy off for them. In reality, this was a precursor to the payroll systems most hospitals have in place now where staff have to similarly tap on and off.

During my brief sojourn at the Masonic, we had a hospital open day where a number of us staff were present to show visitors interested in seeing what it was really like in an operating theatre environment.

I enjoyed giving the visitors we had that day a glimpse behind the curtain of operating theatres. The open day was to show off to locals the changes to their little local hospital, which included the four new operating theatres.

I think we even had a jumping castle in the car park to attract families with kids. This was very novel to me since it was not something I had ever had or expected to see at a public hospital.

This was my first taste of seeing the types of things the private sector did to attract patients, though I still had little understanding of the fact that doctors and patients had to choose to go to the private hospital, whereas the doctor got a public hospital placement where he could work and patients without private health insurance were at the mercy of public hospital waiting lists. Back then, I did not realise how very different those two cultures actually were.

At that time, staff could step out of NSW Health for a period of time and as long as you went back to NSW Health within twelve months, you did not lose your continuity of service, so your long service leave, etc. were not impacted and you got them all back if you re-joined the public sector in time.

I am unclear if that is still an option for staff, but I can attest that it was a good way to draw us back into the public sector. With that in mind, as well as running from the terror of being promoted too soon in what I still considered 'the big smoke', I applied for and got a job at Concord Repatriation Hospital in the theatres.

My brief period at the Masonic was also a positive, if short, experience and I certainly did not leave feeling like I had left anything unsaid. For my sit-down review with myself about the Masonic, my responses are brief, in line with the period of time I spent there:

1. What did I do well at the Masonic? I started to realise that my skills as a scrub nurse were improving all the time. I got to try my hand at a few different specialties at the Masonic, which was interesting and fun. I also started to appreciate how much we theatre nurses got to build a relationship with a surgeon by working with them every week. Public operating theatres tended to move scrub nurses around through all specialties, keeping them more multi-skilled, whereas private theatres really focused on having that one scrub nurse who knew the surgeon like the back of their hand. The challenge was when you came in later and someone else was already doing the theatre specialty lists that you wanted.
2. What could I have done better? I could have made more of an effort to understand how things really worked in the private sector instead of running away with my tail between my legs. But I was still a baby and had plenty of time to grasp that lesson.
3. What was my major take away from the Masonic Hospital? The Masonic was my first brief glimpse into the private sector and it gave me an impression of penny pinching and pandering to doctors, neither things that I was ready to devote myself to full time. It showed me how much I missed the organisational support and basic systems and processes that were in place in the public sector. The public sector seemed very much more attractive after this brief glimpse.

So, I was thrilled to get an interview at Concord since I had just randomly sent my CV and an application letter seeking employment. I was lucky that at that time, it was rare for a large theatre suite, whether public or private, to turn away an experienced scrub RN.

Having my Royal North Shore Hospital background certainly helped with that. I cannot remember the name of the theatre manager who employed me but remember her calm professionalism, which really impressed my country girl sensibilities. I certainly do, however, remember the indomitable floor manager who I soon learnt really ran the place.

The floor manager started as a scary boss lady but over the period of four+ years (1992-1996) I worked at Concord, she became more like a much-loved den mother.

Concord also ran an operating theatre post-graduate course, and it soon became evident that not long after you finished the course, you got to become a clinical nurse specialist, the next career rung up from a Registered Nurse.

Since I had completed my theatre course elsewhere, at the mighty Royal North Shore Hospital, I was allowed to apply for clinical nurse specialist status after three months full time as a Registered Nurse.

It was clear that in the public sector, becoming a clinical nurse specialist was almost a rite of passage after a period of time, much like incrementing from a Registered Nurse year 2 through to a Registered Nurse year 8/ thereafter—the latter being as high as you could go as a Registered Nurse.

Being a clinical nurse specialist involved having more responsibility like being the floor manager on an evening or on the weekend, as well as being affiliated with a specialty which you showed expertise in.

I got to experience some interesting things in my years at Concord including being a scrub nurse in those early days of laparoscopic surgery. What takes an hour or so now used to take more like four-six or more hours back when everyone was learning, and Concord was at the frontier in all things keyhole surgery.

We had night staff and also rostered weekend staff and since Concord did not have obstetrics, we didn't have nearly as much after-hours work—Caesarean births contribute to a lot of after hour's surgery in those hospitals that do offer obstetrics.

We had a designated emergency theatre, which had a team rostered to it every day in case we had an emergency case such as an orthopaedic fracture or maybe a kidney transplant. What a luxury that was to have a team of three staff waiting around just in case there was an emergency.

The team would help out with meal relief in other theatres but never really had the same workload as those in the other theatres.

It was on a weekend where I got to see the case of the inserted glass milk bottle. It had apparently become accidentally lodged in a gentleman's bottom when he apparently fell on it off a ladder. Yeah, right!

The sight of that milk bottle on X-ray is a sight I will never forget. What had made matters worse was that said gent had used a sturdy bit of wire to attempt to retrieve the accidentally lodged milk bottle, managing to perforate his rectum.

True story—trust me, I could not make this stuff up. What topped it off was the anaesthetist abusing said gent for ruining his day water-skiing. And what was the poor patient most worried about—telling his wife what had supposedly happened. Nurses could write a book about some of the stuff we have seen—oh, hang on! That's what I'm doing.

As a rule, we mostly rotated around through surgical specialties, though once you became particularly skilled in one surgical specialty, you did tend to rotate back and forth between a couple.

I learnt the value of an experienced scrub nurse while working at Concord, particularly when there were so many other hospitals around and no-one ever really knocked one back who came looking for a job, fortunately for me.

I tended to do mostly orthopaedics and rotate to a couple of the others including vascular and colorectal. I know I exercised this once with our den mother floor manager boss when she was looking at rostering me to the eye theatres—I told her she might as well just tell me to my face if she wanted me to leave.

Some scrub nurses, somewhere, love scrubbing for eyes. I was just not one of them. It was bad enough on a weekend if we had a detached retina and realised it was better for the non-super eye nurse to scrub while the one who had a clue, scouted, so she would at least know what the surgeon was asking for—she would do a crash course with which ever one of us drew the short straw and would be right there, directing us throughout the entire thing. I had trouble then seeing the teeny tiny instruments and sutures, God help me now with my current crappy eyesight.

I also learnt about developing rapport with surgeons and anaesthetists at Concord. Yes, they had surgical registrars and residents who would often do any emergency surgical cases but as a rule, they did their weekly theatre lists themselves, with said registrars and residents assisting—it could get very crowded in a theatre sometimes.

The consultants at Concord were much more approachable than Royal North Shore Hospital and there was none of that Mr rubbish. Actually, they were probably some of the nicest ones I ever worked with.

Mind you, they could still have dummy spits and go off at you if you did not anticipate something or have the magic 'thing' in the theatre when they needed it. This was an essential part of being a good scrub nurse—anticipating what instrument the surgeon wanted before he or she needed it.

The better you were at this, the faster and smoother the surgery went, and it did give you a buzz when you got it all really right. The challenge would come in orthopaedics when we started using the Stryker power hoods, which gave the patient extra protection from infection, and frankly, extra protection for us from flying bits of blood and bone.

Orthopaedic surgery could get messy with swinging mallets and power saws around. The Stryker hood included a battery pack we wore like a bum-bag around our waist with a tube that attached up into the hood that enclosed our head and shoulders.

This latter had a clear plastic screen all over our face area and since we were so effectively covered and breathing under the hood for hours was already a challenge, we never wore a surgical face mask under it.

This is a critical thing to consider because I am sure I was not the only scrub nurse who may have muttered under my breath at said surgeon about one thing or another—and oh bugger, when they could see your lips move and ask, "What did you say?"

Correct response always, "Erm nothing."

One particular orthopod who really could be hard work used to go off a treat and I can recall on one occasion saying, "Ok, I stuffed up—there's a gun out in the setup room and you can shoot me with it after we finish this case."

Priceless moment—it totally shut him up on that occasion. I may have used it again on more than one occasion and that surgeon went on to give me a fabulous reference when I was leaving. Sometimes, all it takes is standing up to them once to show you will not be treated that way for the behaviour to stop.

It was at Concord that I fell in love with orthopaedic surgery, also getting my first taste of being an acting nurse unit manager when the orthopaedic nurse unit manager (the nurse manager in charge of that surgical specialty) and more senior orthopaedic clinical nurse specialists were away.

The problem I soon discovered was that once you stepped up to a more senior role, it was hard to go back to being a plebe.

Of course, the problem with that at Concord, and probably most large teaching hospital operating theatre suites, was that the nurse unit managers in charge of each specialty would almost always be there until they died or retired, not opening up management opportunities for anyone coming behind.

This could feed a bit of competition, which wasn't always nice. I had discovered during my time as an acting nurse unit manager that I really liked organising things and that I was actually pretty good at it, plus I must admit I liked the extra pay too.

Concord theatre was a fabulous place to work, and I made some really good friends during my time there. Some of them are probably still there, as astounding as I find the thought of never leaving somewhere for the entirety of a career.

I kept in contact with some for a number of years but sadly, when you become busy with your own life and geographically remote, it becomes harder to maintain such connections and they drifted by the wayside. No longer in contact but always fondly remembered.

The girls at Concord taught me how important it was to have a strong team and how much you could achieve together. I made one of my best friends of that time there, the fabulous Suzy, who ended up in Melbourne after a trip with my hubby and me to the Melbourne Cup.

Suzy met her future husband one night as we pub-crawled back to our hotel! Again, geography put paid to that friendship though we have randomly touched base over the years, picking up where we left off and thankfully, finally connecting on social media.

I also spent some of my years at Concord undergoing IVF to try to have a baby, although I suspect no-one there knew about it. I became very good at ducking out for supposed home emergencies or fitting appointments in around my shift work.

We tried IVF for some years without success and I have no doubt that my later career trajectory was in no small part due to this fact—I ploughed the energy and focus a child might have received into my career.

As my hunger for a more senior role grew, I started to peruse the *Sydney Morning Herald* employment adverts each Thursday—this was the day and place where you would find all the nursing jobs of note for Sydney and surrounds at this time. (Circa early 1996) obviously pre-seek.com. And there I found the perfect job for me—it was the orthopaedic nurse unit manager at St George Private Hospital in Kogarah.

Basically, what I was doing at Concord but being a nurse unit manager and in charge of the orthopaedic specialty with St George Private Hospital having four theatres constantly doing orthopaedics, unlike the one theatre at Concord.

I had by this time started doing the occasional ASEPS theatre nursing agency shift on my days off from Concord. I would usually do a 6-hour morning shift, which gave me great extra pocket money but still left the majority of my days off to enjoy.

This was also a great way to suss out what other theatre suites were like. I had completed at least one shift at St George Private, so I knew it was a lovely, shiny, new looking private hospital with a relatively large theatre suite, with friendly staff from what I could recall from my agency shift.

Not all theatre staff treat agency staff well because I guess there is a bit of resentment that the agency nurse gets to just do their allotted shift and leave, not hang around doing all the other clean-up work usually required. So, I was excited to get an interview for the position I applied for.

My interview with the director of clinical services (like a director of nursing but the term more often used in the private sector because it included all patient care related staff, not just nurses) and the perioperative services manager—in charge of theatres, CSSD—where instruments are sterilised, day surgery and endoscopy, changed my mind-set about the private sector and drew me strongly into their orbit.

Both were exceptional female leaders and I like to think I learnt something from both of them. It was this pair that taught me about the need for customer service in the private sector.

I learnt very quickly that if a doctor or visiting medical officer (VMO) as they were called in the private sector, told me to jump, my correct response was 'how high' (tongue in cheek, of course).

It sounds horrifying today in this time of equal rights, but this is the reality of what it was like and to a degree, probably still is. And now, private hospital leaders will sprout defensively about how VMOs have a code of conduct and how they are expected to abide by it, but the truth is executive staff are still expected to surreptitiously say, "How high?" Piss a high revenue earning VMO off at your own peril!

Leaving Concord after four years was scary and thrilling. I loved my years there and took away only good memories of my time working there. My review showed:

1. What did I do well at Concord Hospital? I learnt how to take on more responsibility as well as narrowed my field of surgical scrub expertise to orthopaedics. I had become a pretty good orthopaedic scrub nurse thanks to the generous learning environment I was in. At least, I like to think I was.
2. What could I have done better? I certainly could have been nicer about the eye surgery option—nah, I just couldn't. Bluck!
3. What was my major take away from Concord Hospital? That once you step up to a more senior role, it is very hard to step back and remain fulfilled and happy in your role.

Needless to say, I was ecstatic to get the job, and this move to the private sector was much more successful than my first foray to the Masonic in Ashfield. I started at St George Private Hospital following a full orientation day that included the director of clinical services speaking to us about customer service.

What a novel idea I found this whole customer service focus after working in the public sector where we basically did not really care what the surgeons whined about and it was not uncommon for the nurses to tell the doctor to go back to their poky little private hospital, the latter of which they all usually also worked at, if they wanted some special treatment.

It was well known that they chose which private hospital they worked at, but really did not have much control about which public hospital they had a role at.

What attracted me to St George Private Hospital was that it was part of a large private hospital group called Health Care of Australia (HCOA)—and this group kind of reminded me of being a part of a large public area health service, so I felt way more secure than I ever had at the little stand-alone Masonic.

I soon learnt the arrogance of public health nurses and the difference between a hard day of work in a public hospital and a private hospital theatre suite. At Concord at that time, if you were the evening floor coordinator at about 2, you would walk around the theatre suite and joyfully slash through any large theatre cases that would not be finished by 4pm.

We never gave much thought to those poor patients who were slashed from the list and who needed to then be rescheduled. We were like theatre cops who were determined that no-one worked a particularly hard day despite the fact that there were multiple staff that started at 10.30am to relieve staff, as well as more at 12.30pm and one later evening shift.

Evening staff did not routinely scrub and finish theatre lists—no, we all had a great time doing the set-ups for the next day. Such a waste of resources when I look back but pretty bloody cushy and great fun at the time.

Cue the private sector—talk about a shock to my system! Every theatre, and there were ten of them plus a lithotripsy room at St George Private at that time, had a morning list and an afternoon list.

But where the morning operating theatre lists had to finish by 12.30-13.00, the afternoon operating theatre lists could go until it finished whether it be 6, 8 or 10pm. And the hospital staffed for that.

There were no excess of orderlies to do all the cleaning between cases like in the Concord theatres; oh no, we got in and did that shit ourselves. And certainly, no-one dared to pipe up with a 'that's not my job'.

The turnover between cases in the private sector was astoundingly quick compared to what I had been used to! The hospital organisation structure was also much more appealing to a new nurse unit manager.

I reported to the perioperative services manager who reported to the director of clinical services, who came under the hospital chief executive officer, who reported to the group boss.

No multiple layers of useless roles where no-one ever sees them. I barely set eyes on the director of nursing at Royal North Shore Hospital or Concord and would have had trouble picking them out of a line up, whereas I soon had a relatively friendly relationship with the director of clinical services at St George Private—it helped that we were both grotty little smokers at that time, no doubt.

That relationship contributed so much to how my future played out—I thank you, director of clinical services (Queen JD), if you are still around and hear of this. This director of clinical services called a spade a spade, and as I have always had a similar personality, I am fairly certain that contributed to why we got on.

My role as the orthopaedic nurse unit manager in the theatres at St George Private Hospital was fabulous. I spent my time organising the equipment for theatre lists for the orthopaedic surgeons and developed pretty good relationships with most of them.

I did not routinely have an operating theatre list that I scrubbed for, but I backfilled when someone was sick or double scrubbed to help teach newbies, something I loved doing.

I was also a strong preacher of the theatre nurse catch cry—see one, do one, teach one! That pearl of wisdom is probably still valid today. I shared an office with the educator some of that time, and it was a good time.

St George Private was pretty new and had been the result of closing and combining a number of smaller hospitals, so again, I had landed on my feet in a great work environment with a great team.

The perioperative services manager was an amazing leader and she shaped so much of how I became as a future theatre leader. Her gentle calm approach with a steel backbone was a great role model—she was always perfectly put together and shaped how I thought a private hospital leader should be.

The educator at that time also convinced me to think of further study—as an old hospital-trained Registered Nurse I had veered away from this because I did not want to have to do a bridging diploma, which was common at that time before I could then do what I wanted—a master's in some type of management.

She did all the leg work and found out that I could receive recognised prior learning for my years of work and the theatre course I had completed, so I could enter directly into a master's course.

She also encouraged me to think about where I might want to be one day; something I had not really ever been encouraged to do. My perioperative services manager and St George Private Hospital then supported me doing this, which was amazing.

Most of my subjects were managed in weekend blocks to facilitate working nurses. I commenced my master's in professional studies with a management major at the University of Technology Sydney in about 1998—a course that took four years.

This qualification consisted of all course work and assignments, no sit-down exams. Being in that environment, no matter what subject you study, contributes so much to helping you become a more measured thinker that can consider more than one side of an argument.

It also teaches you that right or wrong, you can find evidence to support pretty much any argument you wish to put. All of this helped to build my confidence and no doubt made me further think I was the bee's knees. I know, I was still having myself on! But they were fun times!

It was while I was at St George Private that I was diagnosed with hyperthyroid or overactive thyroid disease. In my role as the orthopaedic nurse unit manager, I did not routinely scrub for orthopaedic lists unless a member of the usual scrub team was off—managing equipment needs and prosthesis kept me that busy.

In NSW at that time, it was the hospital's responsibility to organise loan sets for joint replacement surgery and woe betide the poor unfortunate scrub nurse, or me, if we didn't get it right.

I was astounded years later when I moved to Queensland to learn that up there, the surgeon organised his own bits and pieces—what a fabulous shock that was. It was also common practice to utilise a scrub nurse as a surgical assistant if the surgeon had been unable to organise their usual assistant and since I was often available, I would end up scrubbing to assist.

Normally, I actually enjoyed it as I am sure most scrub nurses do since you got a much better view of what was going on in this role without the pressure of keeping one step ahead of the surgeon.

As a bit of background, my hubby had been telling me that I was shaking in my sleep and in true obnoxious nurse mode, I kept telling him not to be ridiculous. However, there came a day when I was asked to assist a gynaecologist with a laparoscopic (keyhole) surgical procedure with a major part of my responsibility being to manage the laparoscopic (keyhole) telescope and camera and ensure the gynaecologist could see what he was doing.

That would have been fine if I could have held the bloody camera still—my tremor was exceedingly evident as the view on the monitor shook continuously despite how hard I tried to stop it. Looking back, it was hysterical really; shame the surgeon did not think so.

In true surgeon form, the gynaecologist got a tad upset and yelled at me to find someone else to hold the camera and a sub was quickly sourced—some poor enrolled nurse got the pleasure, I think.

It was after this that my wonderful perioperative services manager suggested I should get myself checked out by a doctor and questioned if I had considered that I might have a problem with my thyroid.

In typical nurse obtuseness, it had never occurred to me that I had anything actually wrong with me. My inability to hold an unwavering telescope triggered my trip to a doctor (GP) that afternoon.

After a check-up and bloods, I went home thinking I was fine, only to receive an urgent phone call that evening from my GP telling me that I had an acutely overactive thyroid and that if I felt at all unwell, I should go immediately to an emergency department because my risk of a thyroid storm (where you can end up in a coma) was high.

Meanwhile, my GP was madly calling around to find me an endocrinologist. Long story short, I very quickly had a partial removal of my thyroid gland with the intention that the bit left behind would provide sufficient thyroxine (get up and go hormone) to manage moving forward.

That sadly never worked, and I have been taking Thyroxine daily ever since. I was offered the option of having radiotherapy but in typical theatre nurse form, I insisted they just cut it out.

Those good days in St George Private were the beginning of showing me how affluent private hospitals were and how—yes, they could make money, but they knew how to spend it on their staff too. At least they did back then.

I got to attend the annual orthopaedic science conference each year I was in the orthopaedic nurse unit manager role starting with Perth soon after I started, followed by Cairns and Canberra with the majority of each of these sponsored by orthopaedic companies—one would pay my registration to conference, one my accommodation and one my airfares—this was back before the Therapeutic Goods Administration (TGA) put a stop to this.

We had been all set to go to Thredbo with my orthopods organising a trauma conference the day of the Thredbo disaster. It was horrifying and those of us that missed the week in the snow were so happy when Stuart Diver was found—it helped us get over our individual disappointment and guilt over missing out, which was pathetic in comparison.

Some of my colleagues at other hospitals actually still went and hung out with the emergency workers down there—we would have loved to still show our support down there but those of us at St George Private had a job to do if there was no legitimate conference to attend.

I also learnt during these times that the private sector knew how to throw a party with the hospital throwing an anniversary ball at St George Leagues Club—we were all dolled up in our ballroom finery and had a truly fantastic time of it.

All staff, VMOs and partners were invited, and it promoted relationships with our doctors that you did not often see in the public sector.

As a part of my support to all of our orthopaedic surgeons, I ended up being roped into running a weekly joint replacement seminar where I basically gave an hour-long lecture, which covered what happens to cause knee and hip problems and I would run through what occurred with a knee replacement and a hip replacement.

This was driven by one of the key orthopaedic surgeons who worked at the hospital, although my talk pushed people towards our website where all of our surgeons were listed. The hospital ran a regular advert for the seminar in the local newspapers around Kogarah and we usually had a full room of interested people.

My biggest challenge was being ready to respond to some of the questions which had obviously originated from Dr Google. To ensure a seamless process when I was away, I trained up one of my key orthopaedic scrub nurses to do the session and to scrub for said orthopaedic surgeon.

It was no surprise when he eventually stole her to be his travelling scrub nurse and work in his practice, which is what often occurred with theatre nurses. I had an offer or two to do the same thing over my years scrubbing but never wanted to narrow my work field down so much, so always politely jokingly declined.

I had been in my orthopaedic nurse unit manager role for a couple of years when I had a similar experience to the one I had with the theatre nurse unit manager and clinical nurse specialist all those years ago in Grafton.

The floor manager under the perioperative services manager had resigned and one afternoon, the director of clinical services and perioperative services manager sat me down and suggested to me that I should consider applying for the role.

This was gobsmacking to me because I really had not thought about doing anything but the orthopaedic nurse unit manager role, despite having started my uni course.

Thankfully for me, they saw something in me that I had not even given thought to—my potential to be a nurse leader.

After getting over the shock of the idea of it, I jumped in without another thought. Again, by luck or their planning, I got the job.

Under the perioperative services manager, I learnt about staffing a private hospital theatre suite with ten theatres and a lithotripsy room. I learnt about the importance of getting the right scrub team with the right surgeon, and the right anaesthetic nurse with each anaesthetist.

It was not potluck like often seemed to happen in the public sector, oh no! Each theatre team was carefully thought out to ensure the best theatre outcomes for that surgeon and their patients.

I learnt to think on my feet and juggle staff to fill gaps where needed, all while keeping our very valuable surgeons happy.

I started by sitting down with all of the theatre staff in individual meetings to look at where they currently worked and where they might like to work if given the chance—this was something I thought of doing because it had occurred to me that it would be easier to staff if people worked where they wanted to and backed up in theatres where they were keen to learn.

It was also a good way to get to know all of the theatre suite staff, some of which I had had little to do with cloistered in my orthopaedic theatres. Thankfully, there was a day surgery nurse unit manager and a CSSD manager who effectively managed their areas and only came to me or the perioperative services manager if they had a drama.

Probably one of the more memorable challenging things I faced at St George Private occurred one day when I had a scout nurse walk out of a theatre because a doctor was rude to them—hello! That is what unfortunately routinely happened in theatres!

You can't treat doctors like they are some forms of demigod and then not have some of them start to believe it. I had to put on my big girl pants and do some juggling to ensure someone was in that theatre working as a scout nurse.

It was a valuable lesson in negotiating with people to achieve the outcome you desired. More like I bribed whoever I could for the favour I would then owe, what can I say? You did what you had to do to get the job done.

I can remember phoning staff and begging them to change their shift or do an extra shift and offering the soul of my firstborn; an ongoing joke! I know this barter system still happens today and I am unsure how that will work with the current labour government's plans to introduce workplace law restricting employers from contacting staff out of hours.

Oh well, I'm sure there will be a consent form for staff to sign, saying they waiver this to cover this restriction on normal private hospital practice. Back then, I quickly learnt that being the floor manager was not that much different than being the orthopaedic nurse unit manager—I was just organising staff instead of equipment.

Another lesson I learnt at St George Private came while I was still working with the orthopaedic surgeons and included discovering how VMOs in the private sector truly spoilt their teams when it came to Christmas.

Admittedly, their wife or practice manager did the purchasing but whoever it was, they had excellent taste. I received everything from expensive bottles of perfume to Clarins gift sets, as well as multiple bottles of wine and boxes of chocolates.

Many would gift me a separate gift for being the orthopaedic NUM who organised their stuff as well as something that could easily be shared with some of the other orthopaedic staff like chocolates, boxes of cherries or mangoes.

It was during my time at St George Private Hospital that my hubby and I made the hard decision to give up IVF after some years—I was about 36 by then and I said I did not want to spend the rest of my life trying to have a baby.

The truth was that we had been coming to terms with this decision for some time as we had failed to succeed with that magic 'just one is all we want' baby, so it was almost a relief to let that dream go.

The reality was that it was easier for us to accept than probably some of my relatives. So, we became cat people—oh, that's right, we already were by then! Then later, dog fur babies took over and that continues today.

Sadly, in about 1998, my perioperative services manager, the best manager I had ever had to that time, was headhunted to go and set up the theatre suite in the new North Shore Private Hospital.

This was one of my first lessons about the power of the head-hunt. She called us all together to tell us her news and we were all devastated that she was leaving but again, another lesson to me from this was that no-one is irreplaceable, no matter how fabulous they are.

Our next perioperative services manager was an older kiwi lady who had been a director of nursing in a previous life in New Zealand. This role was her way of getting a step into the Australian healthcare management sector.

This perioperative services manager taught me about how to performance manage staff—she was really good at it, and it is a skill I took away with me from her, at least according to subordinates that have witnessed me in action or learnt this skillset from me.

As became the norm for my form to date once I was settled into the floor manager job and had acted in the perioperative services manager role when she was away, I began to think that maybe that could be my next step.

The old rule about it being hard to step back once you have stepped up was still in play. My perioperative services manager was very supportive and so it came to pass that I returned from annual leave to be told by her about the perioperative services manager job being advertised at Prince of Wales Private, one of our fellow HCOA group hospitals.

The role had closed the previous Friday, but she encouraged me to send an application anyway on the Monday. A few days later, I received an invitation to go over for a chat with the director of clinical services and the chief executive officer.

I remember I freaked out and even asked my current director of services what that meant; was this an interview? She responded, "They know everything they need to know about you, Fiona, they just want to see if you fit."

Well, talk about no bloody pressure! So, I toddled off over to Prince of Wales Private and spent an hour or so having a lovely chat with the director of clinical services and chief executive officer—two of the nicest managers I ever had the fortune of working with.

We talked about everything from the footy to family—it remained the most pleasant interview I had ever had. A few days later, I was invited to lunch with them in Centennial Park at the gorgeous outdoor cafe where they proceeded to offer me the job as perioperative services manager over wine and food. Still the best recruitment process I had experienced ever!

My move from St George Private to Prince of Wales Private was unlike my previous role changes because of the fact that I was moving within the HCOA group, so although I was leaving the hospital, I was not leaving the group.

It meant that I was off over to the new hospital very quickly with little time for farewells at St George Private because in a lesson I experienced more than once, the more senior role was always deemed more important.

The lessons I learnt at St George Private were too many to list. I had become a well indoctrinated private hospital manager with a very good understanding of how things work in the private sector thanks to the perioperative service managers and the director of clinical services at St George Private. My review showed:

1. What did I do well at St George Private Hospital? I learnt how to manage a private hospital operating theatre suite and build those key relationships with our surgeons. I also learnt that there was much more to a private hospital then just the theatre suite where I had started to see the importance of supporting our VMOs in any way we could to build their business with us.

2. What could I have done better? About this time, it probably would have been timely to sit down and actually think about where I wanted to be by when with my career; however, I was still like a bit of flotsam, blowing wherever luck would send me. A key piece of advice to any aspiring nurse leader is that you need to do an annual review of your goals at each year end; really think about where you want to be and what you need to do to get there. I was doing ok still but I cannot say that I had much control over where I was ending up.
3. What was my major take away from St George Private Hospital? That the private sector rocked and that once you have started in management in a private health group, you will not likely want to go back to the very different hierarchical public sector. It was now 1999 and after starting at St George Private in 1996, I could not envisage ever returning to the public sector.

All I can say is that it really wasn't all on me that I developed a bit of a big head—hell, when you get recruited like I did at Prince of Wales Private, how can you not feel special?

But a lesson I have learnt well is that all good things come to an end, and it was not long after I started that my new chief executive officer, the best chief executive officer I had experienced to date, resigned because he had been appointed as chief executive officer with the Mater group.

To top it off, HCOA had entered the Smedley years and was going through a re-branding as Mayne Health with the red dot, like Target, we all thought.

They appointed a new chief executive officer at Prince of Wales Private, and I then experienced a culture shock change in management styles. Whereas the chief executive officer that appointed me via the garden restaurant would come down to my theatre manager office and put his feet up on my desk and ask, "What's happening, Browny?"

The new chief executive officer would approve something and then after I had ordered it, turn around and tell me I had to cancel the order. He would tell me I had to cancel surgeon's theatre lists, something that had always been under chief executive officer's oversight.

When the surgeon then lost the plot, this chief executive officer would benevolently backflip and give them their theatre list back.

I suppose he sometimes had little more control over some things that he did then I did and just may be simply following head office orders, but it was a quick lesson in how to appear to have no integrity, particularly to the doctors and sales reps that we were stringing along every day. It was around this time that I started grinding my teeth in my sleep—who knew stress could do that to you?

Being the perioperative services manager was an easy step up for me where it just seemed to be a change where I went from organising staffing as the floor manager to one where I was now organising theatre nurse managers (floor managers, etc.) and had more involvement with the VMOs and became a part of the hospital department head team.

It was amazing to me that we would have a monthly department head meeting where the chief executive officer would go through how the hospital was doing financially and what challenges we were facing. It was great to feel a part of that bigger team.

Prince of Wales Private did not have as many social events while I was there—I remember that we apparently could not have money for a Christmas party due to the Smedley money crackdown or something like that and I think the joint theatre and VMO one no longer happened due to staff and VMO drunkenness and other issues at a previous one. Just my luck, I figured!

The roll-over to the year 2000 and the dramas of prepping for Y2K occurred during my arrival at Prince of Wales Private Hospital. It was great to be a part of the group where, much like in a public health area health service, standardised policies and procedures would be disseminated to everyone in the group, making managing the upcoming prep for y2k doable.

It was as much of an anti-climax to us as it was to everyone else when we clocked over to 2000 without anything amiss occurring. And of course, 2000 was the year of the Sydney Olympics—my hubby and I decided to escape Sydney for a good stretch of it and headed west to my eldest sister's wheat/sheep property.

We figured we could live without the dramas of the extra traffic and people generated by the Olympics, although my sister Janis and I made it to a hockey game that we thoroughly enjoyed watching.

Throughout all of these busy moments, I was settling into my perioperative services manager role under the new micro-managing CEO.

What Prince of Wales Private did have was some arrogant as hell surgeons, not least of which was a particular neurosurgeon who was early into his career then but already driving those of us in management to distraction.

He would organise to have patients come in from Vanuatu and practically pick them up from the airport himself and bring them to the hospital to try to operate on them straight away.

If he could not get theatre time during the week, he would bribe the theatre scrub team with actual cash to get them to come in and then rock up to my office with bottles of good red wine to bribe me.

He was just charmingly obnoxious back then, not yet committed to Star Wars neurosurgery where he would go where no-one else had been before or would dare to go. I also had a fabulous stature challenged orthopaedic surgeon that we called the missing link, because the joke was, he dragged his hands on the ground when he walked.

This sounds terribly disrespectful but please be aware, this was a man who would scream in rage at staff in his theatre when something did not go his way or scream in rage at me. Yes, I had no problem stretching to my full height to tower over him as he puffed and carried on.

There were many surgeons I met over the years that we figured only still had a marriage and friends because they only behaved like utter arseholes with us—we knew that if they had behaved like they did with us in civilised company, no-one would tolerate their presence or poor behaviour.

Prince of Wales Private also gave me a crash course in managing human resource emergencies and showed me that I definitely was not in Kansas (Grafton) anymore.

One afternoon, I received a phone call from the police, telling me that they had one of my nurses that they had arrested on a train in Cabramatta buying drugs. Then on another day, I received another call from the police because one of my recovery ward clinical nurse specialists had been pulled over and in his car, he had multiple ampoules of Hypnovel.

Hypnovel is the drug they give you in day surgery when you are having a colonoscopy (black snake) or similar and it has an amnesic effect—the reason why you often don't remember the details of your procedure even though you were awake through it.

All I could do in both cases was confirm that yes, up until then, they did indeed work at my hospital. The third drug issue was a doozy—we discovered that one of my really experienced exceptional clinical nurse specialists had stolen a script pad from one of the surgeons she scrubbed for, and she had been forging herself pain relief scripts.

Further investigation demonstrated that she had ongoing acute back pain and pain medication addiction following a back injury she had experienced some months earlier. I knew the injury was real because I had visited her in the adjacent public hospital when she was a patient.

Her value to us as an employee was supported by the fact that we did not report her to the police since the surgeon she had stolen the script from and who had discovered the issue did not want to pursue charges against her. My director of clinical services, the surgeon, and I decided to support her through rehab and save her job for her.

This was my first lesson that just because someone makes a mistake, it does not mean they are non-salvageable and that sometimes, you should just be a good human being and help them out.

I suspect if this had occurred in the public sector, she would have been suspended while they did some big dramatic investigation and reported her to the police with the final outcome her losing her nurse's registration and ending up with a criminal record.

The latter would have been a tragedy when she really was an excellent nurse. And I heard in later years that all of these aforementioned drug issues were just the surface and that drug deals regularly occurred in the Prince of Wales Private theatre hallways. Naive me—absolutely!

Meanwhile, I received a phone call from my previous director of clinical services from my St George Private time telling me the perioperative services manager role was available at St George Private and she wanted me to apply.

My lovely old kiwi boss had gone onto a more senior executive manager role at Nepean Private Hospital, I think. I thought it was a little icky to go from being the perioperative services manager at Prince of Wales Private for five minutes back to the hospital I had just left, but I loved St George Private, and I really respected my previous director of clinical services as a mentor, so I dutifully presented myself for interview to the current director of clinical services—who had been a ward nurse unit manager when I was there.

My old director of clinical services was, by this time, working as a group director of clinical services at Mayne Health Head Office—what HCOA was now branded as.

The current director of clinical services and I did not really click, which may have been due to the fact I had worked with her when she was a ward nurse unit manager, and we were both basically plebs, plus she probably did not like having me shoved at her—but that was ok—I knew I could do the job they were talking to me about and it was closer to my home—a win in my book.

I figured we would grow on each other after we started working together. But then, instead of quickly hearing that I was successful, I heard nothing for weeks. Remember, technically, they called me, not the other way around.

As luck would have it, I then received a phone call from the human resources manager at Alpha Healthcare about the perioperative services manager job at Westmead Private Hospital, another shiny new private hospital.

Alpha Healthcare was a much smaller private hospital group but still had eight hospitals, so I still felt relatively secure. By this time, I was so unhappy at Prince of Wales Private and Mayne Health and was sick of waiting to hear about St George Private that I gleefully went to meet the Westmead Private Hospital director of clinical services.

She was a delight and proceeded to show me around the hospital and the lovely shiny relatively new theatre suite to see if I would be interested in the role. When I agreed that I was, I had a more formal interview shortly after with the director of clinical services, the chief executive officer, the group human resources manager and a surgeon that was the chair of the medical advisory committee.

I found out after I started that the finance manager, who I had worked with at St George Private Hospital, had suggested me for the role—my first lesson in learning that in the private sector, it often is not what you know but who you know.

Back then, I thought I was pretty special to get a head-hunt phone call, but in later years, came to the realisation that some recruitment companies may just google all of the similar organisations and find out the names of the staff member they are after before calling them to garner if they would be interested. I know—cynical much!

After being offered the role of perioperative services manager at Westmead Private Hospital, I promptly emailed St George Private Hospital and withdrew my application for their perioperative services manager role, stating I had accepted another role.

Within minutes, I had received a phone call from my old mentor director of clinical services who was extremely pissed that I was not waiting for the St George Private job—she told me she hoped I was not making a big mistake.

I had to admit that I agreed with her. I also quickly provided my resignation to the chief executive officer at Prince of Wales Private who I could not get away from fast enough.

The Prince of Wales Private director of clinical services told me later that he had tried to get her to come down and talk me out of it, but she had pushed back and basically said, "No, she has obviously given this move plenty of thought and it is her choice to make."

I really appreciated her doing that—she was a gem and left not that long after me unsurprisingly. Our bloody original

Price of Wales Private Hospital chief executive officer had ruined Prince of Wales Private for both of us.

A life lesson I learnt here was to always remember that if someone came to me with a resignation letter then the correct response was 'Thank you for your service, good luck with your future'.

I forever paid it forward and would never try to talk someone out of resigning with more than one staff member learning that using their resignation as a threat to get what they wanted was never going to work with me.

With such a brief stint at Prince of Wales Private, there was no big farewell or going away fun—I simply worked out my notice and left.

What would I have said to the CEO if I had a chance without repercussions—simply 'stop micro-managing everything and everyone' and 'stop appearing so lacking in integrity—do not say yes to something and then backtrack and say no'. And 'for the love of God, do your own dirty work; that's why you get paid the big bucks'.

I could not get away from Prince of Wales Private, or by that time, the group Mayne Health, fast enough. My review likely reflects that:

1. What did I do well at Prince of Wales Private Hospital? I learnt how to manage some really challenging human resource issues, in particular drug related issues. I restructured the suite which was challenging since the second-in-charge and other managers I inherited were not thrilled with the process. Managing them was as much of a challenge

as some of the other issues. I cannot guarantee I did it well.
2. What could I have done better? I could have tried harder to develop an effective working relationship with the new chief executive officer. I was too busy being silly about what I did and did not like to look at the changes in any positive way.
3. What was my major take away from Prince of Wales Private Hospital? That I really did not enjoy being micromanaged. Perhaps this was some flow on from my Aquarius personality and approach to life; we are very much identified as being loners that march to our own drum. I also now understood that all private hospitals and private healthcare groups were not created equal—some were much better to work for than others. Or rather how the leadership at the top of an organisation can change the culture of that company and not always in a good way.

I jumped into my role as perioperative services manager at Westmead Private Hospital pretty much following the rule book I had learnt at my original St George Private perioperative services manager's knee—even down to installing a large white staffing board on a wall in the theatre suite.

I had done the same thing at Prince of Wales Private, copying what we had at St George Private because I knew that this made staffing in the suite so much easier. I would fill out the board for the week with red gaps for where I would need agency staff and then, often as not, staff strolling past looking at it would put their hand up for a shift here and there.

The reality of nursing staff then, and probably more so now, was that many of them only worked part-time. Often, they only worked enough to cover their child's school fees—paying for childcare was expensive and not all staff thought it was worth the trade-off.

Having one of my current staff nominate themselves for an extra shift was a way more price effective way of staffing than the agency nurse with all of their overheads. These whiteboards have probably now been replaced by spreadsheets on monitors or some similar technological advance, though I would question their effectiveness.

I also again met with all of the theatre team, everyone not just the nurses, in the same way I had done previously—this really was a great way to get to know staff and I would recommend any new perioperative services manager do it.

I restructured and put in place the roles I knew worked to make a theatre suite of any size a success—all copied from St George Private Hospital and my old queen, perioperative services manager.

These included the floor manager, an evening coordinator, a recovery and day surgery NUM and an anaesthetic NUM and last but far from least, the key role of CSSD manager.

I created an awesome team around me, and we really did rock—I arrived in 2001 and felt like I had finally found my niche. It was hard to believe that I had actually only spent 10 months at Prince of Wales Private—I felt I had learnt a lifetime of unpleasant lessons there about honesty and integrity, not to mention the plethora of HR challenges I encountered.

I had learnt the head-hunt lesson well from my own experience and had stolen the evening nurse unit manager and CSSD manager from St George Private Hospital to work with me at Westmead Private.

I then proceeded to steal the educator/neurosurgery clinical nurse specialist from Prince of Wales Private to set up the neuro specialty for me. Within twelve months or so of his appointment, the original floor manager had stepped down from the floor manager role and he stepped up to it.

I had a male educator too and at one stage, I know there was a bit of a joke in the wards about Fiona and her boys—three of them, I think, including the educator. It was not by design, but I was a firm believer that if the best person for the role was a bloke, then so be it.

Trust me—they bitched as much as any girls, so it wasn't for any lack of oestrogen as sometimes was suggested. I had taught the evening nurse unit manager to scrub for orthopaedics at St George Private when he was a baby nurse and loved being the starting point of what I knew would be an amazing management career for him.

At different times after working with me, I know that they all went on to bigger management roles—I will put my hand up for the tiny bit of credit due me for giving them their first management role.

I like to think they took something from me in the same way I took skills from my original perioperative services manager and director of clinical services. Of course, it could be just more of that unbelievable arrogance that I probably still hadn't shaken. Ce la vie!

The team of managers I developed around me at Westmead Private Hospital were the beginning of me understanding the importance of having the right people in those management positions under me.

I was only just starting to truly appreciate that in a way they are your skills resource—for example, my background was as a scrub nurse, so although I had done anaesthetics in my theatre course all those years ago at Royal North Shore Hospital, it was not my thing.

I needed the brains and skillset from my anaesthetic nurse unit manager to truly understand anaesthetic related matters. And this time and role was the beginning of understanding how that team could make me, or any other manager for that matter, look really good—you just have to respect them and let them do their jobs.

So, life lesson here is let people do what they do well! And let them receive the credit for whatever they do—you stealing one ounce of it is the lowest of the low.

Throughout my time at Westmead Private Hospital, I finally finished my Masters in Nursing at the University of Technology Sydney that I had been completing over the four years working at St George Private Hospital, Prince of Wales Private Hospital and then Westmead Private Hospital.

It was four years well spent and I really did benefit from the coursework, which encouraged us to look at healthcare as a big picture. When I graduated, I was sure I would never do anything so time consuming ever again—famous last words.

I started at Westmead Private Hospital in early 2001 and within a few months, all of us department heads were summoned to the boardroom to hear the shocking (and terrifying) news that Alpha Healthcare had been purchased by Ramsay Health Care—another smallish private hospital group that had about 15 private hospitals at that time.

My only knowledge of them was that they owned North Shore Private Hospital where my hero, perioperative services manager had ended up. She actually contacted me to tell me how great Ramsay were to work for—a very smart ploy if anyone suggested it—I promptly told the other department heads to relax and that we were all going to be alright.

And we were—the good news for the majority of us was that the main people to lose their roles in takeovers like that were chief executive officers and sometimes, directors of clinical services, not department managers like us. Thankfully for us, our great director of clinical services survived the spill, and we ended up with an amazing acting chief executive officer for quite a lengthy period as we transitioned into being a Ramsay Health organisation.

She was my first female chief executive officer and was normally part of the strategic management team at head office, but she was also an excellent leader who helped us settle into Ramsay Healthcare with little drama.

We all welcomed Ramsay Health's ownership of us, and it seemed that they had lots of money to throw at whatever we needed. I am sure it was Ramsay Health that funded the neurosurgery specialty expansion at Westmead Private—up to $1m plus for equipment including specialty operating tables, specialty instrumentation and equipment.

Ramsay Healthcare also had something else amazing that continues to this day I expect—they had leadership at the top that really believed in building an excellent staff culture—the Ramsay Health chief executive officer (now, role is called managing director) at that time was an amazing leader who walked the walk throughout his time at the top and waxed lyrical about the Ramsay way, or the way Ramsay Health staff were expected to do things.

It promoted honesty and integrity and all those feel-good things that made you proud to work for them. We used to joke about having our Ramsay Health microchip inserted into the back of our neck; it was a joke. We only half believed it hadn't really happened. That was how well they had orientated us to their culture.

It was at Westmead Private that I learnt about the shades of grey—yep, potentially fifty of them—there often are in management.

I remember at one of my annual performance appraisals that the director of clinical services had told me that on occasion, I was too black and white and I had responded that unfortunately, it is probably a trait from being a theatre scrub nurse who learnt very early that it was either sterile or it was not, there was never any 'maybe its sterile'; if there was any doubt, it was considered contaminated and thrown out.

After this conversation, I started to try to look at things from more than my fixed idea of things. I would like to think I improved but who knows?

During my years at Westmead Private Hospital as perioperative services manager, I had the luck of employing an exceptional scrub enrolled nurse that had completed a theatre training course in New Zealand.

She actually managed the orthopaedic specialty for me with as much skill as any Registered Nurse I had seen doing it, including myself. However, in NSW at that time, it was taboo that enrolled nurses could scrub because that was the more glamorous role for the Registered Nurse in the theatre—it was ok for them to scout but not to scrub.

So, in true 'poke a stick at it' style, I nominated and presented at a theatre conference in Melbourne with a presentation called 'Enrolled Nurse Instrument Nurse—why not?'

Well, I did indeed set the cat among the pigeons, at least for the NSW public health crowd. It actually wasn't as big a surprise to other state representatives at the conference. I particularly loved that I had a number of photos of my enrolled nurse orthopaedic queen in all her scrub regalia with a total joint replacement setup as well as some of Registered Nurses' setup similarly and I asked them to spot the enrolled nurse.

Of course, they couldn't because there was nothing to differentiate them. And the truth was that as long as there was a Registered Nurse in the theatre as the scout or anaesthetic nurse, then it was fine from a legal perspective. Hopefully that old sacred cow has long been put to rest in NSW.

At Westmead Private, I further learnt about the difference between the appointment of clinical nurse specialists in the private sector to the public. It was apparent that in the private sector, we appointed clinical nurse specialists more sparingly and they actually fulfilled the requirements of the role more appropriately.

For example, in the theatre suite, each specialty would have a clinical nurse specialist who looked after all things to do with it. It was only in the case of major sized specialties, like orthopaedics at St George Private, that a nurse unit manager would be appointed.

This flowed through to the wards too where a nurse unit manager may have three or four clinical nurse specialists that would relieve them, be in charge on alternate shifts and have other portfolio responsibilities.

This meant that when a clinical nurse specialist moved up to a more senior role in the private sector, they were generally much more prepared for it. It provided the value and kudos to the role that was not always present in the public sector when you incremented to it just because of how long you have been there.

Westmead Private Hospital also gave me a lesson about managing a VMO's poor performance—I had little choice when one of them managed to punch his fist through a wall in a fit of rage at one of my theatre management team. I had to make it very clear that this type of behaviour was not ok.

It no doubt remains a challenge for many healthcare managers in the private sector—how do you pull a VMO up about their behaviour in such a way that they listen to whatever you are saying and do not pack up their bag and leave altogether. Fortunately, in my case, this VMO realised he was in the wrong and he was embarrassed about the entire thing.

Throughout these years at Westmead Private Hospital, I had been growing into a confident perioperative services manager and had also had an opportunity to act as the director of clinical services a couple of times when she was away.

It was actually quite normal for the perioperative services manager to relieve the director of clinical services in private hospitals because usually, they were considered the next most senior nurse in the facility, and they were also on salary, so it made money sense too.

As much as I got to relieve the director of clinical services and include that on my CV, I cannot say with any honesty that

I really got to do her job. Yes, I got to swan around the hospital doing rounds but I'm pretty sure the executive assistant had more power during that time than I did.

Still, in much the same way as what had happened with my earlier roles, once I had acted up as the director of clinical services, it was hard to go back to just being the perioperative services manager.

I had received a couple of recruiter phone calls by this time to see if I was interested in theatre management roles at other organisations—and as flattering as it was to be called, I declined, saying I was looking for a different role now.

I started giving out the names of my direct reports because I knew their next step might be as a perioperative services manager.

Westmead Private Hospital director of clinical services by this stage knew of my interest in a more senior executive level role and encouraged me to apply for roles. I was more than a little dirty that I did not get her role when she was finally promoted to chief executive officer at the hospital and our acting chief executive officer returned to head office with the role going to a guy from elsewhere.

I knew later that this was actually the best thing because I saw how much better it is for an executive manager to come in fresh from elsewhere with no preconceived ideas of how they are or old relationships from when they were a junior manager—staff just don't respect you as much as the director of clinical services or chief executive officer if they knew you as the ward nurse unit manager or plebe.

My ego was still in great shape at this stage because my theatre management team constantly told me how great I was—oh, how mighty the fall would be when it finally came.

In 2003, Ramsay Health circulated an advert for a deputy chief executive officer at their Hunters Hill Private Hospital. It was the perfect opportunity to be trained as a baby chief executive officer in a baby hospital and I more than met the criteria, so I eagerly applied for it.

I went off on annual leave and proceeded to have my phone interview for the role sitting in my swimsuit in the car in the Crescent Head Caravan Park. The interview seemed to go really well, and I was pretty happy with how I thought I had done.

But then, I returned to work and heard nothing. I then had my director of clinical services at Westmead Private approach me and ask me had I applied for the director of clinical services role at North Shore Private Hospital.

"No," I said. "I was waiting to hear about the Hunters Hill job."

"But I really think you should apply for this director of clinical services job, Fiona."

"So, you are telling me that I am not going to get the other job."

"No, I am just saying you should really apply for this job."

I did not need to be smacked any further around the head with a brick—I dutifully sent my application off to North Shore Private Hospital. Within days, I was being interviewed by North Shore Private Hospital chief executive officer and the Ramsay Health human resources manager and was offered the job before I left.

I actually asked was it fair to assume that if I was being offered this job, then I would not be getting the Hunters Hill job—the answer—yes that would be a fair assumption.

So, within a matter of days, I was employed as the director of clinical services and had to move to North Shore Private Hospital.

I regretted not being able to work out my notice at Westmead Private Hospital and being able to properly say goodbye to my staff, but the argument, similar to what had happened between St George Private and Prince of Wales Private, was that the director of clinical services role at North Shore Private Hospital was far more important than the perioperative services manager at Westmead Private Hospital.

By this stage, I think I kind of always expected shit to go my way because I had been treated like a prized employee for so many of my roles—arriving at North Shore Private Hospital in 2003 felt like I had come full circle from doing my theatre course at Royal North Shore Hospital all those years ago.

I found it ironic that I was now working in what was then the car park. And if every other hospital I had worked at around Sydney had thought they were the best—oh no, they weren't—now, I was really truly with the very best.

With its marble foyer and plush carpeting, North Shore Private Hospital was more like an elite hotel than a hospital. What was a little odd was that I was now my hero, perioperative services manager's boss—and I still kind of considered her my mentor until she was relocated to head office to work on group theatre projects.

She agreed in the beginning that it would not be weird for either of us because she had never wanted the director of clinical services job, and it never really was. This recruitment process was also the first time I had felt like a chess piece being shuffled to where the powers that be wanted me, not where I wanted to go.

Little did I know it was getting about time for me to grow up. As for that Hunters Hill role, it disappeared into the ether and no-one was appointed at that time.

So, although I would have loved to have taken a bit of time to work out my notice at Westmead Private Hospital, I was on the move again.

Throughout each of these most recent moves from St George Private to Prince of Wales Private, and then to Westmead Private Hospital and North Shore Private Hospital, Phillip and I had continued to live in Peakhurst, refurbishing our duplex and installing a fabulous pool for what we had hoped would be a source of cooling down on many hot summer days.

My Westmead Private management team organised a farewell dinner for me, which I enjoyed, and I got to keep tabs with most of them because we were all still part of the same private healthcare group.

So, for my review of my time at Westmead Private:

1. What did I do well at Westmead Private Hospital? By this time, I was a well experienced perioperative services manager and I had learnt well how to build a great theatre team around me. I have often thought since that maybe I should have continued my career in theatres and focused on emulating my mentor perioperative services manager who became a perioperative super consultant. But back then, I was still too busy building castles.

2. What could I have done better? I would have benefited from not listening to my own press too much and letting my ego get out of hand as my Westmead team told me what a great manager I was. This is a very important life lesson, people—once you start to think you are really good at something, you need to move to a table where you will find you are no longer thinking you are the smartest one there.
3. What was my major take away from Westmead Private Hospital? More reinforcement of the lesson about continuing to move forward. That once I had started acting as a relieving director of clinical services, it was always going to be hard to stay as a perioperative services manager. Part of this was wanting the challenge that comes with learning something new. Each time I had been in a role for any period of time, particularly with the perioperative manager roles at Prince of Wales Private and Westmead Private, the routine became very similar. The same types of tasks, just different people and places. And each time I went looking for that next role, it was to a large degree because I was getting bored staying where everything was easy.

The chief executive officer at North Shore Private Hospital who employed me, unfortunately met his demise (termination) within the first twelve months I was there—he lied about an issue with the media and sadly learnt that doing this was not ok with Ramsay Health.

I can still recall his horror as he sat telling me about what was going on and kept asking me if surely it would all be alright. I could think of no way to convince him of that when I was pretty sure I knew what would happen—he was not going to be ok.

I then had a period of weeks where we had a female manager from head office come over and kind of oversee me and the hospital—I learnt a really important skillset from her that I took with me from then—to go spread the fairy dust!

What the, you say? Spreading the fairy dust was about going out and around the hospital and being seen by staff. And about telling the staff at that time that everything would be fine! Fairy dust. A great way to put it! I thought.

The new chief executive officer was a bloke from Dubbo who had been the chief executive officer at St George Private Hospital—I thought he was amazing and I loved working with him.

He was a country boy much like I was a country girl and I thought we worked together really well. He even went so far as to tell me I was the best director of clinical services he had worked with and unfortunately, I was spending far too much time listening to him and the Westmead Private gallery, which suggested to me that I should be looking for chief executive officer opportunities.

North Shore Private Hospital was described as the Ramsay jewel in the crown, and it really seemed that it was. Head office was across the road in St Leonard's and everyone from Paul Ramsay to the Ramsay Health Group chief executive officer regularly dropped in for a visit.

This made all of us think we really truly were pretty special. I had learnt another valuable lesson by this time—if it ain't broke, don't try to fix it! So, I didn't—North Shore

Private Hospital was about learning about how to be a director of clinical services.

I really should have paid more attention to what happened to my predecessor, but I was far too busy being pleased with myself.

I learnt I had not only inherited her seat but her role as the organiser of the annual Ramsay director of clinical services conference—I had had plenty of experience over the years at organising and contributing to theatre conferences, so I was not particularly daunted by this. This was just one of the things that I thought made my job more secure.

After conversations with the Ramsay HR manager in about 2004, I decided to do exactly what I had sworn I would never do again—go back to university. My hubby and I agreed that it made sense for me to complete whatever university qualifications I needed while I was still in Sydney—we did picture a day somewhere in our future when we would no longer make Sydney home.

In hindsight, if I had the opportunity over again when I did my first university qualification, I would have completed an MBA instead of the Master of Nursing—I really needed the finance subjects and other parts of an MBA, which are far more helpful at executive level than a healthcare focused course. So, life lesson, peeps—when looking at post-graduate study to get you to an executive leadership role, do an MBA.

The HR manager helped me locate a post-graduate diploma in financial management at Macquarie Graduate School of Management (MGSM)—an offshoot of Macquarie Uni focused entirely on post-graduate management qualifications.

This diploma made up part of the MBA with me completing marketing, human resource management and basic accounting as the core subjects—those of us only doing diplomas, then specialised in our core area, and I had two further finance management subjects.

What doing this qualification showed me was that I definitely had a brain wired more towards human resource management than towards accounting and finance formulae. I actually received the MGSM medal for my HR subject that reinforced this.

I am still amazed to this day that I managed to get through the finance subjects, including the sit-down exams, which, on the whole, were a waste of time unless I was going to be working in acquisitions and completing financial due diligence as a part of that.

They did give me a much better understanding of hospital finance management reports, which had been the goal anyway.

Again, the subjects were catered to people doing post-graduate work while working full time with some subjects managed in blocks over a couple of weekends and the finance subjects a weekly evening class from 6 to 10.

When I completed this qualification, I really was done with university. I completed two subjects per semester and managed to finish the diploma in eighteen months. I was grateful to the Australian Tertiary Education funding that allowed me to use HECS the first time at UTS and then PELS for the MGSM qualification.

Both were soon paid off via my annual tax reimbursements over a couple of years. It helped that I was earning good money to allow me to do this.

North Shore Private Hospital was a lovely place to work, even if some of the staff were a bit hoity toity! My personal assistant was a legend and helped so much in teaching me how to be a director of clinical services—I'm pretty sure she had more to do with training me for the role than anyone else. We are still in contact to this day via Facebook and she will always have a warm spot in my heart.

At North Shore Private Hospital, I learnt about the true decadence that could be available in a private hospital; at least one that was part of a group who valued their staff and did not hesitate to invest money in them both educationally and socially.

We celebrated the hospital's anniversary party at a fabulous spot at Darling Harbour and usually had our annual Christmas party on-site in our auditorium. Due to our proximity to head office, we usually had members of the board join us for our VMO functions, which the latter loved.

It probably contributed to how obnoxious some of the surgeons could be—it was not unheard of to get a phone call from a Ramsay board member because a VMO had rung them to complain about something.

I also got to take my gang of after-hours' managers on a harbour cruise each Christmas, usually on a mega yacht that would participate in the Sydney to Hobart each year—we would spend a couple of hours on the harbour before adjourning to Rose Bay Yacht Club for a very long, very alcoholic lunch.

I was fortunate enough to have a cab charge card that would get me home from wherever I had been attending a work function. I had developed a relationship with a Silver

Cab driver who lived out not far from me in Peakhurst and I could call and book him for any trips I needed.

I would call him an hour before I wanted to go home and he would arrive and text me that he was waiting, then allowing me 10-15 minutes to get to him. This was really helpful the nights my hubby and I took VMOs to footy games when you would walk out of the ground with hundreds of people after transport.

My fabulous driver would park down the road a bit and turn away all comers until we arrived. It was a mutual relationship because as much as he made my life so much easier, he usually got a good fare anywhere from $70-100 to get me home from St Leonards or the city, ending up out near his home.

North Shore Private Hospital was also my first exposure to ACHS hospital accreditation at an organisation level, having only had to focus on what we did at a department level previously.

All hospitals needed some form of accreditation to show that they were regularly reviewed and that their systems and processes were safe and promoted quality healthcare delivery. In the private sector, it is a key component to the hospital receiving appropriate funding with the private health insurance companies as well as maintaining their licence to operate with their state authority.

I did not really get a grassroots level understanding even then because the hospital 'quality manager' coordinated everything, and I managed to get away with only having oversight. I did not realise this was not great until much later.

North Shore Private, also in true hoity toity form, had a VIP room for patients, not that there is such an option in your health fund cover, or at least, there wasn't back then.

What it meant was that patients could opt to pay an extra $150 per night and stay in a 'VIP' room—trust me, this room type fitted in very well on the north shore of Sydney where the hospital was located. What did they get in their very special room—the room was maybe a tiny bit bigger, it had a small table and chairs and a small sofa, making it more home like.

During meals, the catering staff laid the table with a white tablecloth and flowers to make it appear a bit more special. What did I learn from seeing this? That sometimes people really do have more money than sense.

So, it was also no surprise that this flowed throughout the hospital, or to witness mums who would have an entourage accompany them when they were being discharged with baby, with multiple helpers and the nanny helping to carry the three-foot-high floral arrangements from their stay.

It was also not uncommon for us to have a real VIP guest having their baby where we would more likely close off an entire area for said VIP and family, also managing media parked at entrances to the hospital, trying to spy on someone important coming or going.

Another lesson learnt at NSPH was how to think outside of the box when you are under the pump and do not have enough beds to meet demand—this would be when mums would be discharged to a nearby flash hotel for their final night, overseen by a midwife with their bub staying in the hospital nursery—all this to make up for them usually getting a night alone in the hospital café while staff cared for the baby.

Mind you, the café bunged on a romantic dinner for the couple—this was matched with a dinner voucher if they left early to the hotel.

I also got to learn about some of the craziest patient adverse outcomes at North Shore Private Hospital, with one elderly gent doing a swan dive over his bedrail and straight to the floor.

This would have gone much better for him if he maybe thought to put his arms out in the dive and had saved his nose from greeting the ground first. Another 'I could not make this shit up' moment—although by now, I had to report his injury to the NSW Private Health Facilities group as a sentinel event—where a patient had an unexpected adverse outcome or injury during their stay in hospital.

In mid-2006, I got summoned to my chief executive officer's office to learn that the NSW state manager wanted to see me at state head office at Burwood. I was crapping myself, but he said to relax and that it was probably to discuss an opportunity.

He would have known all the details though he never let on. I arrived out at the NSW state head office where I had a conversation with the NSW state manager and one of the head office managers.

They said they had heard what a great director of clinical services I was and that they wanted me to go be the director of clinical services at St George Private Hospital—Ramsay Health had purchased it and a majority of Mayne Health facilities recently and my appointment was part of their wanting to convert them to the Ramsay way.

I talked about how I was keen to look for a chief executive officer opportunity and it was put to me that I would be given such a chance down the track if I did this one thing for them. What can you say to that?

Not much when you are in a room with two powerful men who tell you that other powerful men, including the chief operating officer of Ramsay Health at that time, agreed with them.

I suggested that it was not a great idea to just shove me in the role and that it would appear better if I participated in the recruitment process. And regretfully in hindsight, they agreed.

I should have just let them install me though God knows how that would have turned out; probably not much better than it did.

You see, their entire idea was all well and good except they forgot to tell the female chief executive officer at St George Private Hospital that I was to be her new director of clinical services.

She and I met briefly one evening soon after the state manager meeting for a drink and we really did not click. To such a degree that I went back to North Shore Private Hospital to my chief executive officer and said I did not want to proceed with the recruitment process at St George Private Hospital because I could really sense that the chief executive officer there did not want me as her director of clinical services.

I am sure it was no joy to be a chief executive officer of a facility with one private health group and your own team one minute, and then suddenly to be purchased by a different group and be told, you 'will have' this person as your new director of clinical services.

My gut had never let me down yet and I was attempting to follow it. My hero leader then shattered my rose coloured glasses and essentially told me to suck it up and go and do what I had been told to do.

So, I went off for the interview with the frosty chief executive officer and some other senior Ramsay leaders and I was not one bit surprised when I did not get the job. I had not performed particularly well in the interview and knew it—I just felt really uncomfortable about the whole idea by then.

My North Shore Private Hospital chief executive officer, on the other hand, was furious that I did not get the job and basically said he did not know what would be done with me now. I was shell-shocked and could not believe my job had gone from the best ever with me being 'amazing' to suddenly being unclear about my role.

I had stupidly never considered that my current chief executive officer and head office had moved on with me in their mind and now that I was no longer on the playing board where they wanted me, I had no place on their playing board at all.

I then received a crash course in what it means to be frozen out at the Ramsay leaders' national conference before being called into the office with my chief executive officer and the Ramsay Health HR manager after we returned to work.

There, the HR manager proceeded to tell me about how I no longer fit with the organisation, and they had to 'let me go'. I asked my chief executive officer in amazement how I had gone from being the best director of clinical services he had ever worked with mere weeks ago to this.

The response was a shoulder shrug and 'it's a change of circumstances'. I knew there was no point in arguing or crying, so I held my tongue and my tears and left with as much dignity as I could muster.

The NSW Ramsay industrial relations consultant that I had developed a close relationship with then contacted me and nursed me out of the organisation. I was paid six months' severance as well as all of my other entitlements including pro-rata 5 years of long service, which I appreciated.

I was shattered for some weeks because I could not get my head around how I had gone from being the golden-haired child, almost literally, to this.

I think I went through almost the stages of grieving, working my way through anger to eventual acceptance. A large part of this was due to how very fully I had embraced Ramsay Health and how very loyal I had been to them, only to have this demonstration of how very little loyalty was offered to me in return.

Part of my severance included the provision of an employment company to help me get another job—something I found truly insulting. They did teach me how to ask for the pay rate I wanted though—you give them a range with your minimum in the middle and go from there.

My chief executive officer also agreed to give me a good reference, which I figured was the least he could do. He also ensured that Ramsay Health picked up the tab for my farewell lunch, a lovely affair that my old mentor perioperative services manager organised for me at some flash beachside restaurant. A fitting farewell indeed.

The industrial relations consultant later told me that the chief executive officer and the HR dude had respected how professionally I had behaved as they had sacked me—good for them! I thought.

What really disappointed me was also hearing that I had supposedly been thrown a lifeline at the Ramsay leaders' conference where we played some table game and the Ramsay Health big kahuna, who I knew reasonably well, joined our table—you had to decide if you would save yourself first before the others and then save them or the other way.

I had innocently determined I should follow the airline stewards and put the mask on first before attempting to help others but no, no, no; that apparently demonstrated that I was beyond salvaging as a director of clinical services with Ramsay Health Care.

I think this latter hurt more than anything because I had only ever had a great experience with the big kahuna when he visited, and I could not grasp that something so seemingly silly had in some small way determined my future. But it was what it was, and I needed to get over it.

I have long understood that there was no doubt more to my removal than they said to me that day about 'not fitting'. The IR consultant had mentioned some vague comment to me about an upset VMO and I had recalled a northern beaches VMO whose wife had used our maternity unit—he made a mega complaint and I had met with him and his wife with my obstetric nurse unit manager to discuss his complaint and he was not happy with any of our responses, though the latter were pretty much advised to us by Ramsay head office lawyers.

I would have at least understood this. I had also recently conducted a 360 review with my department heads at North Shore Private Hospital as part of the annual director of clinical services conference—proposed by me because in my stupidity, I still thought I was the bee's knees, and I am sure that some of the feedback from my direct reports was not what I would have received in the same exercise at Westmead Private Hospital with my direct reports there.

When I made the comment about North Shore Private Hospital, thinking it really was the very best hospital in the city when I arrived new to my role, it was made very clear to me by some of the staff that I was possibly not what they had been expecting or wanting as their new director of clinical services—I expect they wanted someone a little more special than me for their very special hospital.

I can also recall a surgeon at Westmead Private Hospital telling me when I announced my new job that I was going to go over to North Shore Private Hospital and no doubt become a little snob too.

I laughed it him and said don't be ridiculous, but you know what—I think it did happen a bit. They say pride goeth before the fall and never a truer word was spoken—I certainly had hit my fall. This was another lesson in learning that everyone in every role was dispensable.

Of course, there is also the option that it was something else entirely—maybe I was just bloody annoying—and that was the reason for me suddenly no longer 'fitting'.

The unfortunate reality is that this is very typical of the excuse used in these types of conversations when they decide an executive manager (usually the poor old fall guy, director of clinical services) no longer cuts the mustard—they usually leave the poor person being sacked, completely in the dark about whatever it was that they did and so, they can never fix it moving forward.

Healthcare leaders out there having these conversations—stop being a Nancy and actually tell people why you are terminating them. Stop the 'you just don't fit' bullshit once and for all.

What takeaways did I have from North Shore Private Hospital—the latter chief executive officer taught me the importance of having regular meetings with your direct reports and being across all that was going on in their departments.

I also further learnt how important it was to be a collaborative manager—my background was as a theatre manager—I had to appreciate and utilise the clinical nurse unit managers for their specific knowledge about their own ward areas. He also taught me that just because someone tells you one minute you are the bee's knees; that can flip on a dime.

I had continued my strong commitment to succession training at North Shore Private Hospital and had ensured that at least 2 nurse unit managers could act as the director of clinical services if I was away—I knew from my own experience with the director of clinical services at Westmead Private Hospital how important that experience could be.

So, it was no surprise to me when one of those nurse unit managers became the new director of clinical services at North Shore Private Hospital—you're welcome! And the other has gone onto bigger and better things, eventually becoming a chief executive officer.

I also appointed the ICU nurse unit manager who went on to become a director of clinical services elsewhere, I believe. I know I am pushing it to take any credit for them, but I will at least claim that I saw the management potential in at least two of them.

I also further fine-tuned my performance management skills thanks to unfortunately doing a lot of that type of work with the IR consultant. He was really good at it, and I guess I demonstrated that if you do something often enough, you become better at it and sadly, it becomes easier to do.

North Shore Private also reaffirmed for me what utter wankers some doctors could be and wow, did we sometimes cater to it—from a group of chief executive officers (including mine) taking a bunch of the high revenue earners to the World Cup of rugby, which happened to be overseas somewhere, I think—to the weekly escorting of surgeons to the rugby, the NRL or the AFL in the corporate boxes.

My chief executive officer usually had this task but he managed to offload it to me a couple of times and I had the unbelievable (and not in a good way) experience of catering to a group of them.

I would drag my poor hubby along, so he could do the bar runs and they would get the shits if we ran out of champagne or food. I remember getting into trouble when I returned to work after one weekend for going over budget one night and my response was, "Oh yeah, you try telling the neurosurgeon he can't have any more champagne because North Shore Private has run out of money." Not bloody likely.

After my experience at North Shore Private Hospital, I lost most of my desire to be a chief executive officer, at least in a major group, since I did not think that letting go of my honesty and integrity, which sometimes seemed to take a backseat when dollars were involved, would be something I was willing to trade-off for the promotion.

On the day I left North Shore Private Hospital, my hubby and I agreed that we would take this opportunity to leave Sydney. Our agreement had originally been that since he had followed me to Sydney, he could pick our next place as long as I could work as a scrub nurse.

Obviously, my skillset had changed somewhat since that agreement some eighteen years earlier, so he missed out on getting to decide. I set myself up on seek.com with a profile that demonstrated my theatre background.

I applied for a number of roles including one as chief executive officer at a small private hospital in Mackay—it was with a much smaller private hospital group that I thought might be ok.

This role included an initial interview and then I had to submit a bit of a strategic plan for what I would do at the hospital. I did all of that and then never heard from them for weeks.

Leaving North Shore Private Hospital was the most traumatic work experience I had experienced at that stage of my career and it sadly flagged the beginning of me needing to learn to lie like a champion.

The nature of the private sector was that you were only as good as your last job, so if I had applied for jobs and told the truth about what had happened to me at North Shore Private Hospital, I would likely still be looking for a job.

So sadly, my hubby and I both got very good at talking about the tree change that had encouraged our later moves.

My review of North Shore Private is as expected:

1. What did I do well at North Shore Private Hospital? I am unclear what I can say I did well at North Shore Private Hospital other than learn how to act like a stuck-up little snot! Who knew that was a skillset? Well, I did by the time I left. I think probably my claim to fame there would have been my succession training skills again. I guess this particular case demonstrates the real risk involved in training someone to cover your role since it definitely makes it easier for the powers that be to dump you and immediately have someone to cover the role while they recruit someone new. I am inclined to think that it is a key part of your role as an executive manager to succession plan your role to ensure that all of those clinical staff that come under your mantle do not stumble just because you have; however, I understand that many choose not to because they do not want to make it easy to replace them. I cannot say I have ever seen a CEO who succession planned their role in any of the senior roles I was in; I guess they all knew something I didn't!
2. What could I have done better? I could have more strategically thought about how I could end up where I thought I wanted to be, i.e. as a CEO. If I had done that for a moment, I may well have actually considered the director of clinical services role at Greenslopes Private Hospital when my then chief executive officer mentioned it was vacant to me and suggested I think about it. At the time, I poo pooed it, looking down my nose that Greenslopes was some wannabe hospital in Brisbane and that the hospitals

up there could not be nearly as clever and amazing as those in Sydney. Bzzzzt that was so wrong! If anything, I would now suggest that Greenslopes should have been Ramsay's jewel in their crown because it crapped all over any of the little Sydney Ramsay hospitals, both in size and probably in clinical excellence. And after moving to Queensland, I soon discovered that the old health private regulatory unit shat all over NSW's version. The latter just had too many to worry about, I suspect.

3. What was my major take away from North Shore Private Hospital? That you really should not listen too much to your press gallery telling you how amazing you are, so that you start to believe the bullshit. A life shattering eye-opening lesson was that I was just as replaceable as all those other poor executive managers I had gossiped about losing their jobs and you really can flip from having an amazing relationship with a CEO from one second to the next. Sit down, shut up and let these more experienced people advise you about where you should aim to be.

So, after grieving the loss of my role at North Shore Private Hospital over a period of weeks, I shook myself off and got on with trying to find a new job and lo and behold, the best job of my career popped up as an option.

St Andrew's Toowoomba Hospital, a stand-alone private hospital in Queensland, was recruiting a director of clinical services and were after someone who ideally had a perioperative background.

It was actually as if the role had been written for me and I had spent my entire career preparing for it. I excitedly sent off an application soon after.

There were plenty of other job options around at the time and I sometimes wonder where I would be now if I had chased one of them instead. There were a number in Victoria, but hubby and I had both agreed that we did not want to go somewhere where we would freeze our buns off.

There were also some director of nursing jobs in Sydney, one of them with Healthscope, the main competitor with Ramsay Health Care. I ignored the latter partly because at that time, Healthscope had a bad reputation for being cutthroat and regularly sacking an entire hospital executive or chief executive officer, director of nursing, and finance manager. Nope—we wanted to leave the rat race of Sydney and find somewhere for a tree change.

I was thrilled to be contacted by St Andrew's Toowoomba Hospital's (shortened henceforth to SATH because it is such a mouthful) executive assistant to confirm I had an interview for the director of clinical services role I was so excited about.

The SATH chief executive officer and the board of governors treated me with the same high regard I had been accustomed to during a recruitment process previously. I know; only because they did not know about the mess of my leaving North Shore Private Hospital.

They flew both myself and my hubby up to Brisbane for my interview and a member of the board picked us up from the Brisbane airport to drive us the 1.5 hours to Toowoomba. He drove us up to Toowoomba and entered town via the scenic Margaret Street, which was lined with flowering jacaranda trees—it was stunning to hubby and me who had grown up in Grafton, home of the annual jacaranda festival.

I then had morning tea with the chief executive officer and a tour of the hospital. The executive assistant dropped my hubby up the Main Street shops and to our accommodation at the beautiful Vacy Hall, an historic homestead style motel offering a gorgeous historic inner city stay.

I then had a long lunch in the boardroom and an extended interview throughout the afternoon with about 5 members of the board. Not nearly as pleasant as my Prince of Wales Private Hospital experience but still not too bad. At least I got lunch!

I was really impressed with the hospital as I was shown around in the morning—it was not unlike Westmead Private Hospital in its size, and it seemed well maintained and well laid out with spacious corridors and wards.

Every person the chief executive officer introduced me to was lovely and welcoming. It was amazing and felt like I was coming home, especially after the jacaranda trees greeting us on arrival to town.

The chief executive officer hailed from Inverell in northern NSW, so was another country boy—I just hoped it would work out better than my last country boy partnership. It was not lost on me that I had been married in a St Andrew's Presbyterian church in Grafton either! It all seemed to suggest I was where I was meant to be!

My afternoon with the board went for 3-4 hours and finally, towards the late afternoon, they relocated me to the chief executive officer office, so they could ring and talk to my referees—North Shore Private Hospital chief executive officer and the IR consultant.

My later understanding was that they talked to them for some period of time and probably asked everything from what I was like as a manager to what I ate for breakfast. No joke, it seemed like that could have happened.

This was pretty stressful because as much as my previous chief executive officer had assured me that I would receive a great reference report from him, it is still another thing waiting for that to occur and not knowing what he would say.

Whatever they both said, it must have been ok because at about 5pm, SATH chief executive officer came out to see me and tell me that they wanted to offer me the position. He had a contract for me to take away and consider overnight.

The board chairman, a local philanthropist and SATH hospital founder, would now drop me down to Vacy Hall and the chief executive officer would pick myself and my hubby up in the morning to drive us back to Brisbane for our flight home. Could I let him know my decision in the morning?

That 10-minute drive with the board chairman that afternoon, God love him for the country gentleman that he was, actually probably took more like 20 minutes. He was a very slow and studious driver—a forerunner for what he was like as a founder and chairman of the hospital and board of governors. He truly was a gentleman from a different time and regardless of my many later experiences at St Andrew's, he remained so.

That night, we perused the offer of employment, and I was happy to discover that their salary offer was the same as what I had been on at North Shore Private Hospital—not something I was sure would happen since Toowoomba in regional Queensland was a long way from Sydney.

So, my salary trick learnt from the post-employment company worked—I thought I could ask for more, but my hubby was, "Don't push your luck and don't be greedy."

Fair call and I agreed and happily signed the contract. I would have kicked him the next morning during our car trip with the chief executive officer if I could have—I had casually asked the chief executive officer how many applicants they had interviewed, and he responded—just you!

Damn, I probably could have got more but I was just really happy to be moving on with my career and my life in a hospital role that seemed to have been designed personally for me.

It was November 2006 by this time, and I accepted the role with a plan to start after Christmas in the New Year. They, however, had different plans and wanted me to start ASAP in two weeks, so that I would be around for all of the VMO Christmas events, giving me an opportunity to meet many of them.

So, in a mad two-week rush, we packed up our life in Sydney and moved to Toowoomba. And on the day we were packing up the last of our gear in Sydney before our final car trip north, I finally received a call from the Mackay Hospital group to discuss furthering my application.

They seemed a little amazed when I stated I had already accepted another job. Life lesson number whatever, if you are in the process of recruiting someone for a key role and you want the person to remain interested in your role—communicate with them!

A short email would do the trick; otherwise, you risk losing potentially great employees. I could have had a very different end to my story if we had headed to Mackay instead of Toowoomba.

My employment package included the generous salary that matched my Sydney rate at that time, my relocation costs from Sydney to Toowoomba as well as rent for three months while we decided where we wanted to live.

Hubby and I had an overnight trip back to Toowoomba in-between to find somewhere to rent. I had promised I would stay a minimum of 3-5 years and ended up staying 12.5 years, so I have subsequently spent a little more time discussing its impact on my life following.

What I discovered soon after starting at SATH was that the board and chief executive officer had neglected to mention a major factor—the hospital was stuck in a type of management contract with a couple of guys from Brisbane, who had set themselves up as 'Brisbane Private Management Group' or some similar name.

They were pulling significant dollars out of the hospital after they had gutted the place with a massive 're-structure' some years earlier. I would not have accepted the job if I had known the full situation before I started—even I was not that desperate.

I found the concept of supposedly having to report to one of these fellows who was calling himself the director of nursing a bloody joke since as far as I knew, I already reported to the chief executive officer.

I am sure the board would disagree with my description of events; however, the staff all could not wait to tell me their opinion about what had happened, which was not positive. The chief executive officer and the board called it the 're-structure that had to happen'.

I personally would have called it bullshit! Staff told me they actually made roles like the quality manager redundant, made managers stop doing annual staff appraisals; all sorts of basic good hospital management processes.

What was really sad was that within a short period of time, the roles they had deemed redundant had been reinstated by me because an acute medical/surgical hospital that size could not demonstrate best practice without them.

And certainly, could not survive without full ACHS accreditation—another thing they neglected to tell me during my interview—that they only had been given 12 months accreditation and had about 24 recommendations.

Ramsay Health had taught me very well about how an excellent acute private hospital should work and I was appreciative of this knowledge I brought with me.

The good news was that the hospital managed to get out of the management contract within a short period of time and I think the majority of us then tried to forget that that chapter had ever happened.

Although it probably took a good four to five years for staff to stop mentioning it in their appraisal or survey feedback. Even the majority of the board had realised by then that they had stuffed up, though I know the chief executive officer, the board chairman and deputy chair, the likely main instigators of the entire exercise, would never admit it.

Although said chief executive officer freely admitted to me some time later that they had brought in a consultant to do all the re-structuring and sacking because they had known the chief executive officer would not be able to stay if he did it and staff turned on him.

What he also told me unwittingly was that previously, the hospital had a director of nursing who ran the hospital, much like I knew a chief executive officer usually did that role. She apparently had a quality background and had been appointed by the board chairman personally.

Then he was employed as a chief executive officer with no power under her and he proceeded to do a secret review of everything she was doing and reported it to the chairman and deputy chair—who then sacked her.

Unbelievable! In any case, it was all more than enough to make me forget the dramas of North Shore Private and hardly spare them another thought. But it was also enough to ensure I stepped very gently and always tried to keep this new chief executive officer onside.

A very important lesson for any would-be director of clinical services/director of nursing is that you must always have an excellent relationship with your chief executive officer; usually made easier if they were the one to appoint you, because if there is ever trouble at the top of a private hospital, you are usually the one that will be chopped.

I like to think it is a coincidence, and not gender inequality, that the vast majority of director of clinical services/director of nursing are female and the vast majority of chief executive officers just happen to be male!

SATH had a very flat structure and was a stand-alone not-for-profit private hospital. The chief executive officer and director of clinical services reported to the 16-person board of governors and attended a monthly evening board meeting with them.

They met with the finance management group, a sub-committee of the board first and then followed that with the board meeting, usually finishing up about 8.30pm at the latest on the last Wednesday each month.

The reality of the first five years or so I was there was that the chief executive officer and myself met with the board chairman and deputy chair at 4pm on board night and all of the issues and decisions were made at that meeting of the four of us.

Everything then got ratified at the finance and board meeting by the yes people it was stacked with. None of whom would ever argue with the chair or deputy. Coming in from outside, it was almost like everyone acted like the chairman owned the hospital though he actually never did and any money he gave to the hospital, at least while I was there, was always paid back.

SATH was very different from my previous private hospital experience in Sydney because of a number of the services it offered. This included a medical and palliative care ward, which accepted general practitioner (GP) admissions—something unheard of in the acute surgical private hospitals in Sydney unless it was for a week or so over Christmas, and SATH had an acute mental health unit.

I had really only had an acute surgical background, so both of these areas were new to me; however, fortunately for me, there were excellent nurse unit managers in place in both and I really learnt to appreciate the importance of having those skilled knowledgeable leaders in charge of each clinical area.

I settled into my director of clinical services role and got on with again building a great clinical management team around me.

Over the course of my 12+ years in the role, I appointed every nurse unit manager excluding the ICU manager—that young gent was already in his role when I started and was a loyal SATH employee, though no doubt browbeat by the ICU female staff and intensivists.

Other nurse unit manager roles changed due to nurse unit managers leaving town, starting families, stepping back, poor health, retiring and probably other reasons. Were some of them pushed out much like I was from North Shore Private—maybe so!

But the one thing I always tried to enforce was that we termed it 'managing their exit' with them and we genuinely tried to allow the involved person to elect how they were going, i.e. resigning or retiring.

I never escorted someone off the premises in any role I ever worked—there is no reason to do that apart from being an absolute arsehole and the only acceptable reason would involve the police doing the escorting!

And if someone's exit was managed, then there was a good reason, although, sadly, in the private sector, it can be something as simple as 'you no longer have the support or confidence of the doctors'.

When a VMO can pack up their bat and ball and take all of their private surgery to another hospital that can take millions of dollars from the bottom line, sometimes a hospital executive has to make a tough decision to prevent that. Believe me, I got my karma for each of these previous occasions.

I developed a great working relationship with the chief executive officer by learning what I needed to do to keep him onside. He was a micromanager and I learnt early on that it was just easier to tell him everything I was up to, so that he could never accuse me of going behind his back—something

I think the previous sacked quality director of nursing was perceived to have done.

After my experience at North Shore Private, not that I knew what my great transgression was, I was very aware of my need to be on the same team as this chief executive officer.

Our first hospital ACHS accreditation went ok but we still had multiple recommendations and what I learnt afterwards was that the Registered Nurse that had been appointed as the quality manager was way out of her depth and some of what we had submitted had not been as good as it could have been.

Not her fault—all on me really because ultimately, it was in my job description that we passed ACHS accreditation and I had pretty much left her to it, assuming that she had it all in hand. Probably no surprise that she left soon after to seek a teaching career!

Trust me that by the next accreditation cycle, I was all over it, and I never left it all to the quality manager again—it was a massive job and I was ashamed that I had ever left it all to anyone to manage on their own.

The chief executive officer and I quite early got into a routine of going to lunch together out in the staff tearoom—staff learnt they could set their clock by us and find us out there from 12.30-13.00.

It was a great way of cementing our relationship and gave us an opportunity to often fill each other in on whatever we were doing or what we had heard around the traps. When he wasn't being a micro-managing head spinner—the chief executive officer was actually a nice bloke.

I know that he really did have honour and integrity, at least some of the time, because I saw it on plenty of occasions throughout our years together.

All was well for some years but then the great coup of 2011 occurred. The board was appointed and dismissed by the Presbyterian Church of Qld (PCQ)—the reality was that they had no control over the hospital, but they could control changes to the hospital constitution and who was on the board.

In 2011, it came to pass that PCQ decided we needed a hospital chaplain, and one was soon appointed part-time. The next issue that was raised related to the hospital performing termination of pregnancy procedures.

As the director of clinical services, I knew we only performed maybe 6 or so such procedures a year and only on cases meeting the legislation under Qld law. This included babies with anencephalic or no brain and other such major physical abnormalities.

Suddenly, over the course of a weekend, the entire board, excluding some of the good Presbyterians, were sacked and our friendly little PCQ chaplain set himself up as chairman and did a ring around to all of his right-to-life colleagues to replace the sacked members on the board.

The chief executive officer and I overnight did not know if we would survive the tussle and were probably as surprised as anyone that we did some months later. It was a truly messy time in SATH's history with VMOs taking out full page adverts, decrying the church's right to direct their patient care.

What horrified me was the firm belief I had that their action of banning all termination procedures at SATH did not save one baby's supposed life—all they had done was make it more difficult for parents, at a truly horrible time for them, to source appropriate healthcare.

I was just as certain that those parents jumped in their cars and drove down to Brisbane or the Gold Coast or even NSW if that was where they had to go to have the procedure they needed.

An anencephalic baby, if it survived to full term, might survive a few more hours after birth before it died and there were members of the board at that time that thought this was an important thing for a family to experience.

To say I felt rage about some of their patronising beliefs would be an understatement. It was at this time that I had more than one board member, usually one of the four doctors who were included as board members as part of the hospital constitution, tell me that I had to develop a poker face.

Apparently, my horror and disdain were clear to see all over my face. I had to learn to master that and the key I discovered was to look at my notes and not meet other board member's eyes, and to do a lot of counting in my head, although I am not sure I ever fully mastered it.

After months of war, the chaplain chair was booted off the board and a number of doctors were reinstated—this went a long way to restoring the status quo.

The new chairman became none other than the previous chairman's son who happened to be a PCQ elder and who had been on the board for years without making a peep. I am sure I was not the only one surprised to learn that out from under his father's giant shadow, he actually had a voice.

The previous deputy chair accompanied the inclusions back onto the board after being booted in the great sacking—he has continued to perform a role much like a chief operating officer for Ramsay Health, obviously on a much smaller scale.

He became the treasurer, which was apt as he has always been the numbers man that hospital executives had to convince about operational spending and with his experience on other healthcare boards, is likely still the most knowledgeable member of the SATH board.

I loved my job at SATH and really enjoyed helping to bring the hospital back to clinical excellence and ensuring that we had excellent ACHS accreditation status—even receiving 'met with merits' at one stage with no recommendations; a long way from what had greeted me on arrival.

Another proud achievement was convincing the board to allow us to pay wage parity with Qld health nurses wages—it was no easy feat! It single-handedly improved our recruitment and retention overnight. This was maintained throughout my years as director of clinical services, but I would not guarantee it continues—the chief executive officer and some members of the board were always scaremongering that the hospital was close to bankruptcy and could not afford such things, which was often ludicrous, at least back then.

The hospital went from strength to strength; although if you listened to some members of the board or the chief executive officer, we were always on the brink of collapse—not ever really true in later years while I was there.

Whenever they started this narrative to justify not paying the nurses' parity or not buying some piece of equipment a VMO really wanted, I gritted my teeth and smiled. I looked after the nurses and the chief executive officer looked after non-clinical.

If anything, even vaguely clinical came up with him, he called me—because he was 'not clinical' and I quote him, and the hospital medical director, the retired gentlemen general surgeon only worked part-time.

The chief executive officer's background was as an account's person at Inverell Public Hospital before eventually ending up as the NSW area chief executive officer for Dubbo and he had only ever worked in the public sector before St Andrew's.

He always said his contract ran out. Possibly just like mine did at North Shore Private! I was in no position to throw stones. This lack of an understanding of clinical matters came back to bite me big time.

The medical director was eventually replaced by a young vascular surgeon who also only performed the role part-time—unfortunately, issues usually only popped up on their days off.

During the early years, I remember telling the chief executive officer about the VMO entertaining we did at the footy, etc. with Ramsay Health and his public health background could not grasp it—he found the entire idea grotesque and corrupt and could not understand that Ramsay considered it relationship building.

As much as it pained me to admit—it did work—because that high revenue neurosurgeon was more likely to come and give you a chance to fix something after you shared champagne at the footy, instead of throwing their toys out of the sandpit and marching off to another private hospital.

The latter being the constant threat the VMOs held over our heads. Fortunately for SATH, there were only the two acute private hospitals in Toowoomba, and the other one—St Vincent's Private—did not have a lot of VMO support back then. Made the competition much easier.

In April 2015, my personal life was presented with a bit of a challenge when my 87-year-old mum phoned me to tell me she had been told that her abdominal cancer primary was ovarian cancer.

Now, as a nurse, I had learnt that not having children could increase your risk of ovarian cancer, so my ears perked up immediately. I promptly went off to my lovely female GP and asked for a referral to a gynaecologist on-site, so I could have my 'Angelina surgery'.

I had quickly decided that I did not need my uterus or ovaries and should get rid of the lot of them—the old theatre nurse in me coming to the fore. I saw my gynaecologist and rather than do the surgery straight away, I decided to leave it until early December, so it would be easier for me to have time off.

We were about to have ACHS hospital accreditation in June or July, so I was flat out in my role. So, my gynaecologist booked me into one of his December theatre lists and I merrily went on my way and got on with my life.

Then in June 2015, my mum passed away and afterward, I started to think that I was being silly having the big surgery, that my mum was 87 and so on and so on, until I convinced myself not to have the surgery.

So, back I toddled to my GP to ask her to get the surgeon to cancel me from his list. Thank God for her—she refused and told me that if I wanted to cancel it, I had to go and see him and do it myself.

So, I did—by this time, it was probably October sometime. He happily removed me from his December theatre list but insisted I have a pelvic ultrasound to be sure.

I kept that ultrasound request form in my desk for probably a couple of weeks before I finally remembered to get the ultrasound done. Then I heard nothing, so I happily went on with my life assuming that all was ok, or the doctor would have called me.

Then weeks and weeks later, I returned from lunch one day to my executive assistant telling me I had an urgent message that the gynaecologist needed to see me ASAP. My response was, "oh fuck!"

When she asked what was wrong, I responded that something must be wrong or he would not be wanting to see me urgently. It turned out he had been volunteering overseas for weeks, hence the delay seeing my results. Bugger!

Life lesson, peeps—if you don't hear from your doctor after having tests done, do not assume they were ok, ring their rooms and double check! Just to be sure!

What he told me was that my pelvic ultrasound had identified a 3cm lump and subsequent CTs and MRIs convinced him and other colleagues that he consulted that it was a fibroma.

I was even seen by a general surgeon as well and all agreed that they were sure it was a fibroma. And so, on Friday, 18 December 2015, I was in the operating theatres at St Andrew's Toowoomba Hospital, having a laparoscopic assisted total hysterectomy and bilateral salpingo-oopherecromy; or in normal speak, removal of my uterus, ovaries and fallopian tubes.

From what I was told later, there was silence when they got inside me in the theatre because it was quickly apparent that it was not a fibroma and was actually something far worse.

Full credit to my gynae surgeon who actually got on the phone to his gynae oncologist colleague in Brisbane to discuss what he had found and what he needed to do—I never found this latter out until 2020 from that gynae oncologist.

So, my gynae guy and the theatre team then spent hours removing all of my nasty bits and every other little bit of anything they thought could be bad.

As a consequence, I suspect the entire hospital knew I had ovarian cancer long before I did. Because you know, the anaesthetist just happened to be one of the doctors on the board, so he had to go and tell the chief executive officer.

Of course, the theatre staff told their colleagues, who told their colleagues. I do not judge anyone for this because I appreciate what a terrible shock it had been for everyone in the theatre—they were supposed to be doing a relatively simple gynae procedure on their director of clinical services, not discovering such a shocking infiltrator.

My hubby also knew, which I did not discover until days later and it must have been a terrible burden to keep from me—because no-one wanted to give me the really shitty news until it was confirmed by pathology. You know, just in case by some bloody miracle, it was not cancer.

So, I recovered in my surgical room with a view, being spoilt by my fabulous clinical team as my gynae surgeon visited daily and hinted about things but never quite came out and said it until Sunday or Monday when the pathologist confirmed it.

The brutal truth was that I had ovarian cancer that had originated in my fallopian tubes, which is apparently quite common—who knew, and was also in the fluid washings where they rinsed out my pelvis.

There had also been a small spot on my bladder. These latter two things basically meant that I was stage 2 because it had spread but it had not spread too far yet. So, of course, I did the whole stupid Dr Google and had it reinforced to me about how truly shitty this diagnosis was.

On the bright side, I had been diagnosed early and my prognosis was a lot more positive than those unfortunate women diagnosed at stage 4. The sad reality of ovarian cancer remains that due to its lack of early diagnosis tests or even signs and symptoms, the majority of sufferers are not diagnosed until stage 4 when it has already spread everywhere.

There are approximately 1800 females diagnosed with this horrid disease every year in Australia with about 1000 deaths from it each year. Yep—that does not leave a lot of us alive.

Dr Google at that time said I had about a 43% chance of surviving 5 years, so it was truly shitty news. I still thank my mum daily for her saving my life with that phone call.

It was then time for a crash course in stages of ovarian cancer—Dr Google promptly told me that:

1. Stage 1—Cancer is in one or both ovaries.
2. Stage 2—Cancer is in one or both ovaries and has spread to other organs in the pelvis (uterus, fallopian tubes, bladder or bowel). Although, as stated previously, apparently, ovarian cancer often presents in the fallopian tubes.
3. Stage 3—Cancer is in one or both ovaries and has spread beyond the pelvis to the lining of the abdomen (peritoneum) or to nearby lymph nodes.
4. Stage 4—The cancer has spread further to distant organs such as the lung or liver.

Stages 1-2 meant it was early ovarian cancer. Stages 3-4 meant the cancer was more advanced. According to the Australian Cancer Council website, 7 out of 10 cases of ovarian cancer are diagnosed at stage 3 or 4. And a woman's lifetime risk of developing ovarian cancer is about 1.3%

By this stage, it was a couple of days before Christmas and since I had still only had laparoscopic surgery for most of my procedure, I was good to go home. As you would expect, I called by the executive office to talk to my boss and our executive assistant, who was herself a good friend and huge support to my role and gave them my horror news.

My hubby accompanied me because he knew them both well and let's face it, I had just had major surgery. I soon discovered that they already knew thanks to the VMO and nurse grapevine; essentially, everyone knew.

When you have just been told that you have ovarian cancer, one you know is really the deadliest female cancer, you might expect to be a little shell-shocked and it would be fair to say that would describe me at that time.

All I could really say was that yes, I had cancer but that I could not have a PET CT to determine how widespread it was until early in the New Year. I was also yet to see an oncologist. After a brief stilted discussion about potential people doing my job, and how long I was likely to have off, I was very happy to escape home.

My hubby and I then proceeded to have what was no doubt the worse Christmas we had experienced to date in our lives. It is a terrible state to be in when you know you have cancer but do not know how bad your cancer is, has it spread, how long you have got to live.

So many questions I had, and my poor husband had just as many. We made it through a short break over Christmas and I actually returned to work within three weeks—we had a Qld health private regulatory unit audit, and they wait for nobody.

Besides, laparoscopic surgery is amazing—I really did not feel like I had major surgery despite what had happened on the inside. Why did I have to front up for the audit, or why did I delay surgery back earlier in the year because of accreditation, because I did not have anyone to relieve me.

The chief executive officer, for some stupid reason, did not think it was necessary, so for the 12.5 years I was there, no-one ever relieved me as the director of clinical services. I tried many times to be allowed to succession train someone but for whatever archaic reason, he would not agree.

If any of you are reading this, do have a backup plan for your role—stop being so arrogant and succession train someone. You are not irreplaceable, so get over yourself. I really do think many still don't do it because they are scared it will make it easier to get rid of them. Sad but true!

How did I come to terms with the fact that I had the most lethal female cancer you could get? In those first couple of weeks prior to hearing that my cancer had not spread, I wallowed and grieved and did all of those things that you hear people talk about—and then I got some of the best advice I received at the time—one of those aggravating right to lifer doctor on the board contacted me and pointed out very gently that I was not dead yet!

It was a bit like a light bulb moment where I kind of shook myself off and decided that I was going to be ok. And that basically, it was what it was, and there was no point dwelling and fretting on it—neither would change the outcome.

I have been told many times over the ensuing years that I have an amazingly positive attitude despite my cancer—and my response to that is simple. Wailing and screaming 'woe is me' will not change my health outcome.

If anything, all it will do is make everyone around me miserable—it was no-one else's fault that I had cancer. Plus being in healthcare and surrounded by it, I have always had 100% faith in whatever treatment my doctors propose!

I have had family, friends and even a GP at one stage, suggest all sorts of wonder cures or treatments but none of those things ever appealed to me—I knew that medicine was my best bet, and it has not failed me yet!

Did I ever have any of the multitude of signs and symptoms of ovarian cancer that might have flagged that I had this deadly cancer? No, I did not have a single one that I could recall or take note of.

We women have weird, odd twangs and aches in our pelvis as a part of being a woman and I am sure I am not the only one that never gave any of them much of a second thought.

Who knows; maybe one of them was telling me that I had it. This silent killer sneaks up on us when we are unaware and so, we often do not get diagnosed until it is way too late to help us.

So please, any woman reading this, please have a look at the symptoms I have listed and if you even think you vaguely have one of them, go to your GP and insist they check you out for ovarian cancer.

Remember that as the patient, you get to argue and say that, "No, you are not happy," with any diagnosis you feel is not appropriate. If your symptoms persist and your current GP is not helping, you then go and get a second opinion. You are entitled to do this! The earlier they catch it, the better chance of survival you have.

The most commonly reported symptoms from Dr Google are:

1. Increased abdominal size or persistent abdominal bloating. I had no memory of experiencing this.
2. Abdominal or pelvic (lower tummy) pain. I had no memory of this.
3. Feeling full after eating a small amount. Again, I did not recall ever noticing this.
4. Needing to urinate often or urgently. Nope—I had not noticed that either, though I did usually get up at least once during the night for the toilet.
5. Other symptoms included changes in bowel habits, unexplained weight gain or loss, excessive fatigue, lower back pain, indigestion or nausea, bleeding after menopause or in-between periods, pain during sex or bleeding after. I had no recollection of any of these things.

According to information available at cancer.org.au, some of the causes of ovarian cancer or things that can increase your risk include:

- Age (risk increases for women over 50)—yes, this applied to me as I was 53 at diagnosis.

- Family history of ovarian, breast or bowel cancer—yes, this applied to me.
- Changes in the genes BRCA1 or BRCA2.
- Being of Ashkenazi Jewish descent.
- Early onset of periods (before 12 years) and late menopause.
- Women who have not had children or had their first child after the age of 35—yes, this applied to me.
- Using oestrogen only hormone replacement therapy or fertility treatment—yes, this applied to me. I had undergone the IVF in my early 30s and I had started perimenopause in my late 40s, at one stage being so crabby that I finally twigged that maybe I needed some hormone replacement. (Ladies who have experienced perimenopause may well relate to that feeling you have where, if someone looks at you sideways, you really do want to give them a wee feral snarl! It's hormones, ladies; not our fault.) I saw a gynaecologist about this and he started me on hormone replacement therapy, which assisted greatly with my need to snarl.

So, in hindsight, there were a few of the causes that applied to me, not that I was aware of most of them at the time. This website also reports that some things that may reduce your risk include using oral contraceptive pill for several years (I did this), having your fallopian tubes tied or removed, and having children before the age of 35 and breastfeeding.

Early in the new year of 2016, I started with my oncologist and I finally had the much-anticipated PET CT, which showed that they had thankfully got all of the cancer.

I started chemotherapy after the required break post-surgery (you need 4 weeks either side of surgery to ensure the chemo does not impact your surgery or your healing) with a plan to do four months, then have a break, so I could go down to Brisbane to the gynae oncologist to have major abdominal surgery where he would cut me from sneezer to breezer, as my mum would say. Not quite but close.

The surgery would include debulking my pelvis and abdomen, removal of my omentum and removal of my appendix—all of which would have occurred initially if anyone had realised it was cancer before my first surgery.

Then have another two months of chemo to finish things off. The initial proposal was that I have three months of chemo, then the surgery, then the next three months of chemo—I delayed it again to fit around some work-related matter since the gynae oncologist assured me that doing so would not be an issue.

Before I started anything, I was back into hospital as a day patient to have a port-a-cath inserted to my chest to allow easy chemo administration.

I regrettably had a vascular surgeon do mine who obviously had little experience at that time with them since my port-a-cath was placed so that the wound was directly across the top of the port instead of burrowing the port over to the side of the wound like the general surgeon who usually did them always managed to do.

This meant that mine could not be used for my first 3-week cycle of treatments because nurses would have had to stab my still painful wound. I believe the vascular surgeon changed this practice following feedback from my oncologist—one would hope so.

Those initial days of treatment involved a few challenges including the fact that I was recovering at home on the 40-acre property where we had built a new house in 2008 on my own.

Phillip worked for Ergon as an electrical linesman and worked away for 10 days at a time. I had to drive myself into town for my treatments and home afterwards—everyone was concerned about my ability to do this, but I was fine.

My fur babies, Jack and Jill, our Jack Russells, had managed to get themselves bitten by a brown snake just before my diagnosis, so we were a houseful of survivors at that time. The brown snake did not survive the encounter and it appeared neither had my ovarian cancer, which made us all winners.

With my background as a theatre nurse, I had not had much to do with oncology but fortunately, we had a brilliant team of oncology nurses. They, along with the SATH managers and ward staff, wrapped me up in a massive caring hug and nurtured me through all of it.

I survived it all relatively unscathed except for losing my hair due to one of the chemo agents (Paclitaxol), which was nothing a wig did not fix, and a little bit of chemo brain—which was not too bad that first time round.

I chose to wear a wig throughout because I personally felt that as soon as you see a woman with one of those snug turbans on their head, you assume they have cancer. And that person is treated differently as a result.

My wig was great and I did not need to admit I had cancer to anyone unless I wanted to. Did I sometimes respond, "It's a wig," to people complimenting my hair for shock value? Maybe so; sorry, I am only human.

I also amassed a collection of elasticised headbands that I used to wear every day—people probably thought I was being a bit vain but the reality was that having the elasticised headband made the wig feel more secure and like it could not just randomly fall off, flashing my poor shaved skull to all and sundry.

I had been taking Phenergan of a night for my sinusitis for years and I swear to this day that continuing to do so helped prevent me from being really sick like you hear happens with so many people—because guess what wonder drug they give you in oncology if you have a reaction to the chemo drug—you guessed it, Phenergan.

Last but not least, I cannot forget the menopause I was kicked back into and the lovely night sweats I suddenly experienced—I still smile when I recall the advice my oncologist gave me when I told her—with gestures, she said, "Simple, Fiona, sheets on (gesturing pulling sheets up) and sheets off (gesturing pulling them down)." Works just as well today as it did then.

My attitude then became totally focused on the positive—stage 2 ovarian cancer relative 5-year survival rate was something like 78%. That was awesome compared to what I had been imagining. And only something like 4% were diagnosed at stage 2, so I was really lucky—I decided to focus on gratitude too.

Gratitude to my mum who had saved my life—I was so grateful that she thought to tell us in that April 2015 phone call about what her doctor had told her about having an ovarian primary cancer, I was also grateful that she did not live to see me diagnosed—she would have probably blamed herself for something that was nothing to do with her—we were both just bloody unlucky.

I also decided early in my ovarian cancer experience that I was going to share my journey on Facebook—my Facebook friends are mostly family with a few friends and I really wanted to ensure that the story that got out and spread around the dining room table was my real story.

This was where I found the group 'Happy to be alive', which really resonated with me at that time and I quite possibly flooded my Facebook feed with positive quotes such as 'Always find time for the things that make you happy to be alive'.

The one that I decided was going to be my mantra was 'No matter how you feel, get up, dress up, show up, never give up!' I appreciate that some people will really struggle to find that positive thought, but I really believe that you become what you think about.

So, if you think you are fine and you are doing ok, then you end up being that way. Another quote that continues to empower me and support my theory that thinking positive thoughts truly helps with positive outcomes was 'your mind is a garden, your thoughts are the seeds. You can grow flowers, or you can grow weeds'.

Never a truer word was written, I think. I felt that if you start down the rabbit hole of thinking about your cancer and your prognosis and where you will be in the future, you will end up falling into worry and stressing about your future and every other little thing you think of.

I guess it might equate to the whole placebo effect where you are actually fooling your body into thinking it is ok. I am living testament that it works—my doctors were often surprised throughout my journey that I recovered so easily from the surgery and did not get really sick from the chemo, and I managed to work full time throughout. As a cancer survivor, I tried very hard to only focus on the positive wherever I could.

The amazing group called 'Look good feel better' came into my life in early 2016 also. They are the free national community service program that is run by the 'Cancer Patients Foundation', which is dedicated to teaching cancer patients how to manage the appearance related side effects of chemo, in particular hair loss.

Because SATH had a large oncology unit, this group used to use the hospital's boardroom for their monthly sessions and would organise access to the boardroom through my executive assistant who informed me one day that she had booked me into the next session.

When I said I didn't want to go because I knew how to use makeup, she convinced me by telling me I would get a show bag—what can I say—I am a sucker for a show bag! I am so glad that I did because it turns out that I knew how to do my makeup when I still had eyebrows and eye lashes—they taught us how to draw on realistic eyebrows and how to use eye liner to give a pretender of having eyelashes.

One of the local hairdressers that specialised in sourcing wigs and doing the fitting, etc. also came to the meeting. There were probably about 6 of us cancer sufferers in that meeting and it was a mixture of confronting and comforting because those ladies could truly relate to what I was going through.

Our age range was extreme with our youngest in her 30s and the oldest in her 70s. So many stories of different types of cancer, including another woman with ovarian cancer who caught up with me afterwards—I felt guilty when we exchanged our stories and stages of diagnosis when I was stage 2 and she was stage 4, only being diagnosed when she bumped her belly on her kitchen bench and it hurt her.

It broke my heart to hear that the lovely older lady I had bonded with had pancreatic cancer, a dreadful aggressive disease. I would like to think that my joking and positive attitude rubbed off on them a little.

But, back to work we go and fortunately, after all of the good news in the New Year, which supported that I was not going to drop dead anytime soon, the chief executive officer and the board backed off and let me get on with doing my job, offering me whatever support as needed to do so with no further mention of someone replacing me.

In my first few weeks back, we received feedback about the rumour mill running rampant at the other private hospital in Toowoomba, so I decided to send an email to all staff to counter it.

I clearly explained what had happened to me and spelt out that I was undergoing treatment and I was fine. Not dying; at least, no more so than anyone else. It was only the very early part of my experience that was messy but to be fair, it was a terrible shock for all of us to come to terms with.

I had my last chemo treatment in August 2016 and according to my oncologist, I was cured. Hmm. Probably should have argued that a bit in hindsight.

I had only one hiccup at this time when I woke up one morning not that long after finishing my last chemo in August 2016 to discover what appeared to be a hole in the incision line over my port-a-cath—remember how I had stated that the vascular surgeon had put the wound on top of the port instead of burrowing it, causing me initial delays with using it.

Well, now that constant pressure from the port under the wound was causing it to come open. Really not ideal to have an open wound to a port that accessed my blood system. So, I called into said vascular surgeon and showed them my issue, and it was no shock to me that by lunch time, I was on the theatre list, having it removed.

So, if you ever need to have a port-a-cath inserted, please make sure you ask the doctor inserting it if they will be burrowing it away from the wound—if the answer is no, then ask that doctor very nicely to refer you to a surgeon who will do it that way, the proper way. I then started my three-monthly follow-ups and routine cancer surveillance without any drama.

During this time, I got to visit a geneticist to identify if I had the BRCA gene mutations; you know, the ones Angelina Jolie made everyone aware of in relation to breast cancer. It was a surprise to discover that the BRCA gene mutations are more prevalent in ovarian cancer than breast cancer, so it was really important for me to find out if I had either.

If I did have the mutation, it would have impacted the cancer risk to all of my female and male siblings and their children, including the boys because it can be passed by the boys onto their daughters.

Before I went to the initial geneticist in Brisbane, I had to map out my family history of cancer for both of my parents and do a bit of a family tree with who had what. I, of course, had my mum with her ovarian cancer and there was also a history of bowel cancer and a few other types within both family bloodlines.

I then would receive points for how much cancer was in my family tree to determine if I would have to pay for the genetic testing or not. If I had needed to pay for it, the price would have been expensive.

I need not have worried because my having ovarian cancer and my mother having it were sufficient to provide all the points I needed. Because I met the threshold for free testing, he then sent me off and told me I would be contacted by the public hospital in Toowoomba to organise my testing. He warned me it could be anywhere up to six months before I heard from them.

Then about six weeks later, they called me and organised for me to go over to Toowoomba Base Hospital to be swabbed for the genetic testing.

While there, I told the nurse that I had not been expecting to hear from them for months and she guiltily informed me that they always triage ovarian cancer ASAP because the grim reality was that if they left it too long, often we ovarian cancer patients were not still around to be tested.

Confronting much! The good news was that my swab demonstrated that I did not have the BRACA gene mutations, a huge relief to me and my relatives.

Throughout my initial treatment, my oncologist was a legend and it is worth mentioning now that her husband was one of our anaesthetists that also worked in the ICU—I thought he was pretty awesome too.

He was, in fact, amazing in December 2016 when my hubby managed to rupture his bowel on Christmas Day and needed a laparotomy and colostomy in Griffith in western NSW.

He was a phone call away and offered me no end of support as I tried to figure out how to get hubby back to Queensland—no easy feat, it turned out. It ended up being a mad dash with me driving from Griffith to Toowoomba with an overnight in Dubbo.

This was a very effective way to get me to forget about my little cancer issue and I did joke to my hubby that he really didn't need to go to such extreme measures to get the attention away from me.

Now, SATH was still chugging away, going from strength to strength, attracting new VMOs and introducing new specialties like robot-assisted surgery.

We were no backwater hospital but a vibrant acute regional medical/surgical hospital that would compete with any similar sized private hospital in Australia, which I knew from my own comparative experience in St George Private, Prince of Wales Private and Westmead Private in Sydney.

We did not have ward RMOs, so medical emergency team (MET) calls were managed by the ICU RMO and ICU staff. As a private hospital, our specialists were expected to provide their own patient care, which they did very effectively.

With no emergency department, we managed to utilise the St Vincent's Private one very well—they saw the patient and then they were transferred to us. Worked fabulously for us, though not so well for them.

One of the other things we did really well over these years was celebrate Christmas—SATH had a long-held tradition before I arrived, which continued throughout my 12.5 years there that involved hospital-wide participation in a very serious (seriously fun) Christmas decoration competition.

Every ward/department participated in the Christmas theme competition with glee and bribes. Each year, the department head would be given an extra amount of $ to add to the Christmas decoration horde they already had.

Managers would submit their theme secretly to the hospital's executive assistant who coordinated the entire thing. One of her many skills that she never really received appropriate recognition for.

We would invite key stakeholders such as the wives and children of new VMOs to come on-site and judge the Christmas decorations hospital-wide. The chief executive officer, our executive assistant and I would accompany them around the hospital as they experienced each area's Christmas fun.

The visit for judging would include bribes for the judges and us, even though we really did not get to sway their opinion. It always fascinated us sometimes about why one area would be selected over another when we would often think another area was a shoo-in to win.

The first prize would be a mega hamper of all sorts of goodies filling a large clothes basket, which could be readily distributed among staff. Second prize wasn't much less, and the winner received an actual trophy with a Santa on it that would be engraved with the winner in the New Year—they got to hang onto it for the year.

So many amazing themes over my years there with a few standouts being the twelve days of Christmas quotes to us by staff as we worked our way around the ward or the bush or

Disney Christmas' in the medical ward with everyone in costume.

We had choirs welcoming us and all sorts of incredible efforts and regardless to who won, everyone got joy out of it. We would have our staff Christmas party following judging morning with a big part of it being the naming of the winner.

Christmas also included every member of staff receiving a gift, which our executive assistant diligently hunted down and sourced each year, everything from a SATH themed drink bottle to a SATH themed umbrella—I still have the latter to this day.

And you know the difference at SATH, in comparison to North Shore Private; for example, where staff even once poo pooed $100 gift vouchers, the SATH staff every year were grateful and thrilled at whatever gift they received. It was like the quarterly BBQ the chief executive officer and I cooked—it really was the thought and effort to say thanks that mattered.

Any new staff arriving to experience either of those things were blown away—such a simple way to say thanks that was lucky to cost a few thousand dollars.

The other bit of Christmas fun we did for the department heads, and yes, us too, which I will take credit for implementing was that we did not do committee or other formal meetings during December.

Most staff are away for part of the month and in 12.5 years, the place never fell down or behind because we did it. It just made December more fun for everyone.

SATH continued to roll along doing well until suddenly the treasurer (numbers man) on the board and the chief executive officer determined that the hospital finance manager, who had been managing all of the hospital finance related areas perfectly fine for years, was suddenly not sufficient for her role.

They determined they needed someone who could do more in-depth financial analysis, something you would associate more with a large private health group head office than a little stand-alone regional private hospital, but it was what they decided the hospital needed.

Before the rest of us knew it, they had recruited a young bloke who was suddenly the director of finance over the previous finance manager who was essentially still doing all of what she did previously.

His primary role appeared to be writing a 60-page uni assignment for each board meeting. The previous finance manager was pushed out in short order.

The director of finance then needed another accountant to do the role of the previous finance manager and basically oversee all of the associated staff, since the new director of finance was not particularly good at interacting with people.

His usual modus operandi would be to sit in front of his multiple computer screens covered in spreadsheets with his headphones in—I never did know what he was listening to but I doubt it was a talking spreadsheet.

The status quo prior to the DOF appointment was that the order of hierarchy was the CEO, then me as DCS and then the FM, although the latter was never really treated as being a part of our executive management team.

In fact, the executive assistant probably held more of that power, appropriately or not. Then the new director of finance started and was immediately part of our executive team, which was certainly what I had been accustomed to in the Sydney private hospitals I had worked in.

I had no beef with this young gent since he seemed like a nice nerdy dude and he pretty much stayed holed up in his office doing his finance reports and stayed away from the clinical areas completely.

It is worth noting that up until this time, the CEO and I had had the health information manager try to convince us that we should look at an electronic medical record (EMR) but the chief executive officer's response was always, "No, we will not be the first, we will wait until most others have them before we look at one," or something to that effect.

All was relatively well with the world at this time until said young director of finance went off to some IT type conference and happened upon a rep who, might I say, saw him coming.

Suddenly, after returning from the conference, we were looking at an electronic medical record (EMR)—he managed to get the chief executive officer and treasurer on board very quickly and next thing, the company was on sight doing scoping work.

The director of finance continued to talk up how it would allow us to reduce staffing and save heaps of money and I continued to argue with him and tell him that it would not reduce nurses since the EMR could not give a needle or assist with a shower.

I know he heard me and yet, he continued to press this with the number crunchers who obviously preferred to believe him than the silly little nurse director of clinical services.

It turned out that this wonder EMR was only in place in non-English speaking countries, so what a good idea it was for us to pursue it—at least, I thought they were crazy but I got the sense very early in the piece from the chief executive officer that I needed to get on the bus or get off altogether.

So, I got on and tried to at least ensure it would meet our clinical needs. Did I knock back the chance to travel to Brazil with the chief executive officer and director of finance to see the EMR in use? Of course, I didn't! Hello, Rio! This was in July 2018.

Although I would highly recommend if you ever make the trip to Rio de Janeiro or São Paulo that you take more than five days to do it—we had a whirlwind trip visiting a few hospitals interspersed with being wined and dined in some truly amazing restaurants.

I had the best steak I have ever had at a gorgeous restaurant in Sau Paulo, which had a giant tree overhanging the area where we ate. Our hosts certainly went all out to impress us.

I was the one that went into any detail with hospital staff during our hospital visits though often that was a joke because we needed a translator.

Again, the DOF did a mega uni assignment on the benefits of the EMR and all the savings he thought would occur. Again, I argued constantly throughout that it would not reduce the number of nurses.

Unfortunately, no-one was listening to me. The boys and some members of the board proceeded to spend days locked away with the company coming up with a contract—I was not invited, so could only assume that the whole matter was far too complicated for a director of clinical services.

So, I stayed out of it and tried to put my 10-cents worth in whenever I had an opportunity, helping to recruit required roles needed to build our on-site EMR. See, SATH got a good deal because the company was using it as a site to build their English version of the EMR.

Numerous lovely Brazilians arrived on-site to assist with this process, and despite all the other challenges involved, they were a joy to work with.

Of course, such issues never occur in isolation that would make our jobs easy! Our wheels started to fall off, or rather mine did, when we started having issues with one of our ICU RMOs.

Nursing staff were complaining about the ICU RMO's behaviour at medical emergency team (MET) calls and physicians were complaining about his behaviour in the ICU.

In amongst all of this, the oncologists were having problems with a palliative care doctor and ICU medical staff were concerned about inappropriate MET calls being called on patients that should have been commenced on end-of-life care and should have had a not-for-resuscitation order in place.

One fine afternoon, the anaesthetist/ICU VMO, my hero anaesthetist, presented to the chief executive officer's office, complaining about the palliative care MET calls. I was in my office, minding my own clinical nursing business when the chief executive officer called out for me to join them in his office because the matter was 'clinical'.

If I had it over again today, I would have responded to him to call the director of medical services and get her in since it was a doctor matter. It should have been her purview not mine as the lowly nurse in executive.

Instead, I was a good little director of clinical services and joined them, and proceeded to have a disagreement with the

VMO when he informed us that the ICU RMOs would no longer attend MET calls for a particular palliative care doctor.

I am sure I paused, expecting the chief executive officer to interject but he said nothing—so, I had to disagree. I stated that I was sorry but that the RMOs would attend all MET calls as it was a part of their job to which I was told, "No, they would not."

Throughout this altercation, the chief executive officer said nothing, not truly helpful from the head of the organisation. I again stated that yes, they would attend all MET calls since they have no way of knowing whose patient it was until they got there.

When further argument occurred, I responded that we might not be able to make them do anything when they got there but we could insist they attend the MET as our employee.

By this time, the full time ICU RMO had been called down to join us. It was a horrible situation that I should never have been put in; however, I felt I had to make a stand for any patient in our care that may need a MET call. This occurred in about 2017, I think; and it was the beginning of my end at SATH.

To address all of the concerns of, by this time, multiple physicians complaining about their access to the ICU and issues they were having with the full time ICU RMO and one of the intensivists, the chief executive officer and the board decided to employ an independent specialist to complete an ICU service review.

An intensive care specialist from a Brisbane facility was subsequently employed as a consultant and spent some weeks on-site, conducting interviews with multiple VMOs and nursing staff.

The physicians made full use of him and spelt out very clearly the issues they were having with ICU. It is of note that the review doctor told us mid-review that I needed to take care because the intensivists were after my scalp—the blame for the review and issues the ICU RMO was having, were placed firmly at my feet.

He also told us that the physicians really felt the exercise was pointless because the chief executive officer would not do anything about the recommendations if it meant rocking the boat. This was a bit like a red flag at a bull for the chief executive officer who then became aggressively determined to take action, perhaps why the consultant reviewer told him in that way.

The action recommended included immediately removing the full time ICU RMO, which the chief executive officer had me do with him. Again, this should have been the director of medical services; however, somehow this role managed to stay out of the entire mess.

Very clever and possibly where the description that this doctor ran with the foxes (us) and hunted with the hounds (medical staff) originated from. It was always going to be a challenging role for a doctor who performed the medical director role part-time and then relied on those same medical staff they were supposed to performance manage for referrals in their private practice.

I appreciate that the director of medical services tried very hard to keep her two roles separate and this was a huge challenge for her, not helped by some of her colleagues.

As anticipated, the termination of the RMO did not go well and ended up involving lawyers, letters, the latter of which the chief executive officer made me write. He signed off on all wording and insisted on some aspects remaining that I had wanted to remove.

The ICU RMO also happened to be besties with all of the consultant medical officers that worked in the ICU even though he was meant to report to and be accountable to them. They did not take this well and again, it was all blamed on me.

I accept that I should have refused to do any of the things I was involved in relating to the RMO—I unfortunately got so caught up in the thought that I was helping to remove this person who bullied my nurses that I lost sight of what my role should have been in it, i.e. no role at all.

For some stupid reason, it never occurred to me to just say no to the chief executive officer—I had been trained too well about where I fit in the food chain and saying no to his role was never part of that training.

You see what I had long come to believe by this time was that my major role as the director of clinical services was to be the advocate for the nursing staff—that it was my job to stand up and in front of my nurses when a doctor was coming for them.

PS: If you want to live long and prosper as a director of clinical services/director of nursing, probably best not to do this. Swallow down that integrity and try not to choke on it.

The second major recommendation from the review was that the full time intensivist in charge of the unit no longer be the ICU director and so, the chief executive officer, and again me instead of the medical director, recruited the ICU director from the Toowoomba Base Hospital to have oversight at SATH too.

The changes sent shockwaves through the hospital, and I am sure a major part of it was that no-one could believe that the chief executive officer had actually actioned the recommendations.

I remain unclear how I managed to wear the blame for the entire mess; however, it would not surprise me if somehow he contributed to that impression, much like he did with the director of nursing back before me, protecting himself at the same time.

To be realistic, he had survived (at least for some period of time) the political games and backstabbing of the NSW public health service, so he was far more accustomed to these games than I was. And he had survived the previous SATH re-structure 'that had to happen'.

To top things off, I ended up being given the ICU RMO roster to manage because our removed ICU RMO used to do this and the director of medical services who should have taken it over, refused to do so.

Her power to refuse was much higher than mine, so I got stuck with the truly thankless task—it was full credit to the new ICU director that this was not a disaster as he helped share/recruit RMOs across both sites.

The recommendation to introduce 12-hour ICU RMO shifts instead of the previous 24-hour shifts was also introduced and made the expectation that the ICU RMO working the night shift was actually available for work instead of sleeping, way more effective.

So, as you might have garnered throughout all of this, far more quickly than I ever did at the time, all of the issues with

ICU had seriously pissed off my hero anaesthetist/intensivist since he was particular good friends with the ousted ICU RMO, and had probably still never forgiven me for arguing with him about the ICU RMO attending all MET calls.

Of course, this had a flow on effect to my oncologist—of course, it would and should have since I was apparently attacking her husband. I stupidly blindly continued along going to my oncology follow-up appointments with her, never twigging that she probably really did not want to see me.

I know—stupid, stupid me. She never suggested that seeing me was a problem and was always only professional during those visits. I am sure they both thought it was reasonable to expect that between her being my oncologist and him being so helpful to me in the past that I should have shown them loyalty and just shut up and let him do and say what he wanted.

Unfortunately, being a 'right fighter' prevents you from doing that. I remain regretful that what followed with the deterioration of my relationship with both was so messy.

Over the ensuing years of 2018-2019, my relationship with the intensivists never really improved although I had always thought that my interactions with the new ICU director were fine and professional and without drama.

Our oncology nurse unit manager decided to transition to retirement and wanted to become a part-time breast care nurse instead—this eventually was sorted out though it was messy at stages due to the chief executive officer directing me about what pay level I could and could not appoint her to—again, as the messenger, I was the culprit.

It is worth noting here that I had been trained to always function as a member of a united executive team—it never occurred to me to run around saying to anyone that this or that were not my idea but the chief executive officer's.

We recruited a new relatively inexperienced oncology nurse unit manager who really struggled with her role—she did not have the support of the oncology staff and it became so messy that I ended up meeting with the oncology staff individually and laid it on the line that their behaviour with her was bordering on bullying.

This was instigated because of an oncologist, my oncologist, presenting in our office, upset about the mess that oncology apparently now was. Not my finest hour but we were desperate to not lose the oncology nurse unit manager since we had not been overwhelmed with applicants, or rather received any other than hers.

She was also finding said oncologist terrifying and was frequently in the executive office with the chief executive officer and me, in hysterical tears about how she did not know what to do and how the oncologist was picking on her. We offered advice and asked her to go away over Christmas and think about what she wanted to do.

In early 2019, the chief executive officer proceeded to tell me that he had met with this oncologist, my still oncologist, while I was on leave, and she had expressed concerns to him that I was bullying the oncology nurse unit manager and the previous one.

He pulled no punches in telling me this and could not quite understand why I was suddenly devastated because my hero oncologist was saying such terrible things about me. I then told him that obviously, I needed to find a new oncologist as a priority though he did not think this was a really good idea.

I promptly returned to my GP where I had an hysterical breakdown while I told her how shattered I was about my oncologist and how in my own stupid ignorance, I should have realised what a problem it was for me to continue as her patient—she gave me a referral to another oncologist, coincidentally one who had a special interest in ovarian cancer, and I started seeing him.

My appointment with him was a revelation. He could sketch the bell curve of ovarian cancer recurrence and show me where I was on it. He did not suggest to me that I was 'cured' and despite what you might expect that was much more comforting.

He also switched me back to three-monthly reviews for a little longer (I had been switched out to six monthly still within my initial three years post diagnosis) since he argued that recurrence usually occurs in that initial three years. It was a relief because it is a little scary when your follow-up visits start to spread out.

Suddenly, around this time in early 2019, the oncology nurse unit manager stopped coming to us in tears about the oncologist or the staff and we assumed that she was finally settling into her role.

In hindsight, what she had likely done was discover that the oncologist really had a bigger problem with me than her and that feeding into that was to her benefit. Over the following months, a terrible game of lies progressed where the oncology nurse unit manager would come and have her usual meeting with me, no dramas, no tears, nothing.

Then suddenly, after she had left my office, the chief executive officer would get a call from the oncologist because said oncology manager was in her office in tears because of her meeting with me and how I had treated her.

My executive assistant witnessed her exit my office, happily smiling and saying goodbye; however, apparently by the time she got down the corridor to the ICU where the ICU nurse unit manager would happen upon her, she was sobbing hysterically.

This was a new one for me in my long career as a director of clinical services and I had never come across a dishonest game player like her before and as a consequence, had absolutely no idea how to deal with her.

It actually got to the stage that I did not want to have my usual monthly one-on-one meeting with her because I knew the performance she was likely to put on afterwards; however, the chief executive officer insisted that I continue to do so.

It is now that I reiterate that I will take on the mantle of a whistle-blower if needed down the track. In about March 2019, a MET call occurred in the oncology department, which the ward RMO attended and then made a comment afterwards to me about the use of Phenergan.

I made mention of it to the oncology manager in an email, referencing how I had believed that part of the reason I never got sick with my chemo treatments was that I took Phenergan every night for my sinusitis.

This was never a drama for me; however, she apparently ran off to the oncologist, my old oncologist and the oncologist involved in the MET call, and I think, suggested that I was asking questions about the MET call.

No, I hadn't been, but suddenly from their reaction, it seemed like maybe I should be. On that same day, my after-hours manager informed me that she had been at the MET call and that allegedly, the oncologist had given intravenous adrenaline instead of intramuscular and the patient ended up in ICU for a brief period afterwards.

Not dead, so really still not a major issue to me. Next thing, I was being bombarded with all sorts of literature and information and suddenly, at the next medical advisory committee, I was attacked for daring to question the oncologist about a MET call.

I still actually hadn't questioned her about anything. Oh, how I wish that back when the chief executive officer told me about the feedback from this oncologist about me that I had just gone and seen her and we had nutted out all of the problems supposedly between us—unfortunately, it was far too late for this.

By this stage, due to ongoing dramas with her husband, in relation to RMO treatment and me calling him on it, I was now supposedly bullying him too. Heads up, all you bullies out there—someone telling you that your behaviour towards someone is not appropriate or appears bullying is that person actually bullying you!

The hounds were baying by this stage, and I should have ran for the hills! I suggested that I should go and meet with the oncologist and her husband together to the chief executive officer and said he and the director of medical services could come, so that we could get everything out in the open and try to diffuse it, but he did not think this was a good idea.

He was sure it would all fizzle out in no time if we just let it alone. This approach probably worked beautifully in the public sector where more likely, I would have been drafted sideways somewhere.

Meanwhile, at the medical advisory committee, which coincidentally both the oncologist and her husband were members of, the chief executive officer and other members were trying to calm the pair of them down who were now demanding my termination for daring to question a VMO's practice—which I still actually hadn't ever done.

It is worth noting here that it actually was part of my purview as director of clinical services to review MET calls for tabling at the critical care forum which I chaired, and a summary of that forum was a part of my monthly board report.

However, somehow, we were reverting to expected practice from 20-30 years prior when nurses were expected to be seen and not heard by doctors. I was quite certain that the office of the health ombudsman and coroner might have something to say about that. So, to attempt to pacify them, the decision was made to have an independent MET call review of the incident in oncology.

This is where it just gets ridiculous—the chief executive officer, on behalf of the hospital medical advisory committee and the board, contracted the local solicitor that worked with the hospital to do the MET call review.

This was a little regional solicitor who had no healthcare experience or relevant clinical expertise. His review included him interviewing the oncologist, interviewing the director of medical services, and interviewing me.

I showed up with a large folder full of copies of emails and meeting minutes and every applicable thing that supported the fairy-tale the oncology manager had been spreading, none of which I suspect he looked at.

Each of us spent probably 1-2 hours with him and then he proceeded to take weeks to present his final findings. By this time, both doctors were frantic for my removal, while the chief executive officer thought that the review report would make it all go away.

About three weeks later, the MET call review report, a two-page letter basically, was provided to the chief executive officer. This pearl of wisdom essentially stated that I, as a nurse, should leave doctor matters to doctors—to say I was gobsmacked was an understatement—this was 2019.

The report was tabled at the next medical advisory committee and did not satisfy the married pair of VMOs now practically screaming for my sacking. I was removed from the meeting, an unheard-of action, to allow further discussion.

After the meeting, a couple of the other VMOs retired to the chief executive officer's office with the chief executive officer and me, where no-one could come up with any solution to the problem.

The accusations about me supposedly bullying the oncology manager were also growing and as a final stand—she resigned due to my supposed treatment of her. By this stage of the proceeding, I was acutely stressed and actually physically unwell—if something like this ever happens to you, be smart—resign and leave long before it gets to this stage.

A sad surrender but far better than making yourself physically unwell out of loyalty to an organisation that ultimately has none for you and will not have your back.

Soon after this, I attended a family funeral interstate and on the Monday I returned, the chief executive officer called me into his office to tell me that he had received a letter from the oncologist, which was also signed by all of the other oncologists, all of whom I had never even had a conversation with, demanding my termination or they would take all of their work to the other private hospital—millions of dollars of work.

She had not been satisfied with the little perceived wrist tap I had received from the MET call review and wanted me gone. He also told me that he had spoken with a number of oncology staff who had accused me of bullying and that he was considering a HR review—to this, I laughed and said, "Oh yeah, like the MET call review with the local solicitor, I suppose—don't insult me."

He then said he had spoken with the chairman of the board and the treasurer, and they agreed with his plan and that he had a meeting down with said solicitor later that day to determine my future at SATH. He then had the hide to say to me that I should never have changed oncologists because that was probably what set her off!

I basically said, "You are fucking kidding me, aren't you!"

Shrug. "Nope!"

I then asked him, "Was that it and should I leave the hospital?"

He responded that no—with a bit of his usual neck and head twitch—as far as he was concerned, I was still employed by SATH, so I was expected to stay. I know—what the! This was at about 9 in the morning.

So, I was finally falling prey to the weight of a VMO's financial value to a hospital, something I knew was always a risk and which I had sadly thought would never occur to me. Karma is a bitch and she got me good.

I should have left there and then but unfortunately, I needed the details nutted out—was I being sacked and if so, with what conditions. This was unfortunately not my first go at this rodeo, but the reality was that this mess had been going on since at least January 2019 and it was a relief that it was finally coming to a head.

I knew I had hung on too long out of loyalty to the hospital and my fantastic clinical nurse team and I was paying the price for that now. But I didn't leave, I visited a number of my clinical managers and told them that I was going and said goodbye and wished them well. I packed up my 12.5 years of life in my office and made a few trips to my car.

The chief executive officer did not have his meeting with the mighty local solicitor until about 2pm and it was after 3 that he finally returned and called me into his office. He proceeded to present me with a piece of paper with his handwritten options on it which included: 1) I resign, and I get paid 3 months' pay (tight arses), I get a farewell and I get a reference from him, or 2) I don't resign, I am terminated and I get no farewell or reference.

There was a third option about a HR review, but I cannot recall the detail of it since it was so ridiculous as an option. He then generously said I could take it away with me and email him my response.

At about 3.15pm, I finally got to take my leave of the hospital that had contributed to some of the best times, and definitely the worst, in my career. Again, I did so with as much dignity as I could muster.

Oh, and oopsie, no deed of agreement for me to sign telling me I could not say anything like I have just finished saying.

Later that evening, I emailed the chief executive officer and stated that obviously I had no choice but to take option one since I needed his reference to get another job, but that no thanks, I would organise my own farewell.

I could not stomach the thought of ever seeing him again. The following day, he called all of the department heads together and told them what he had done—to give him credit, he did not try to pretend that I had resigned willingly; probably because he knew that some of my managers knew the truth of what had been going on.

He even went so far as to state that the oncologist was worth however many millions of dollars and so, he had to do what he did to his old mate; oh yeah—that was me.

Apparently, one of my managers made the query that if he would do this to the director of clinical services over a doctor, what chance would one of them have if they had an issue with a VMO?

His response, I believe, suggested that they don't put themselves in that position to find out. How to trash a hospital's culture and kill their trust in one fell swoop.

As for the crazy arse oncology manager who had played the final card of supposedly resigning because of me, she apparently tried to withdraw her resignation after she heard about what had happened to me—but the chief executive officer refused to allow her to do so because as much as he had used her feedback as a reason to sack me, he undoubtedly knew she was a liar because of all of the copies of emails and other documentation that I had provided to both him and the director of medical services which demonstrated this.

They were both well aware that she was full of shit but chose to ignore it. She got a job somewhere else, with a fabulous reference from the oncologist, no doubt, so if you have an oncology manager, be wary—and just maybe—be very afraid!

I greatly regret that she contributed to the final breakdown of my relationship with my initial oncologist—I know—she was only a part of it, but it was still really disappointing. And guess what, I imagine that the oncology MET call incident never was appropriately reviewed.

The concern to me is that if this type of clinical incident was brushed over so effectively while I was there, what has been covered up since I left?

What did I take from my 12.5 years at SATH? To absolutely always stay the hell away from doctor matters—they are not for you, director of clinical services/director of nursing. Leave that crap to the chief executive officer whether he has the balls for it or not. NOT YOUR JOB! Unless you are protecting a nurse, leave them to it! Mind you, the best made plans don't always work out.

I also knew that I could definitely still grow an excellent clinical management team—I had appointed all except one of my clinical managers at SATH and each had their own skills and personality traits that they brought to the team.

I called them my brain's trust and we all joked about our meeting table being the round table of Camelot. I considered myself a consultative manager and certainly feedback from my managers since supports that—I was more like their wrangler than their boss.

Although, do not mistake that I was the leader—I always tried to be firm but fair and frankly usually used the yard stick as—will someone die if I say yes to this? And if the answer was no, it wasn't against the law, would not cost a mozzah and either contributed to improved patient care or staff satisfaction, then my answer would be yes.

I actually would not have survived the last five months of my role when I was being hunted out of the organisation had it not been for a couple of my clinical managers who discovered what was going on and offered me significant support. I now call the two of them very close friends and I am grateful always for their ongoing presence in my life.

What did I find funny after I left? The board and chief executive officer decided they should change my replacement's job title to director of nursing as if they were sure it was the title of my role (director of clinical services) that helped lead me astray—not an ounce of common sense to realise that the issues occurred due to their chief executive officer dragging the director of clinical services into medical matters, not the other way around.

Unfortunately, from all accounts of staff still at the hospital, the hospital has failed from strength to strength! If that makes sense. But that is another story and not mine to tell!

So then (early June 2019), I yet again found myself looking for a new job. My hubby and I had purchased a gorgeous little Queenslander renovated house in Newtown (Toowoomba) and moved into town in 2017 after eight years out on the 40-acre property 30 minutes from town.

I loved that little in-town house and I am fairly certain that I was possibly more devastated about having to leave that house then having to leave SATH or Toowoomba. The reality of regional cities is that there are simply not enough hospitals for a director of clinical services to easily find another similar job, so I had no choice but to move on.

By July 2019, I had managed to complete at least three interviews for a role as the director of nursing at Sunnybank Private Hospital in Brisbane—the first was with the general manager in a lengthy phone call, then the second, a face to face with him as well as the finance manager, and the acting director of nursing—who was actually the obstetrics manager.

It was the first time I had been interviewed by a peer (finance manager) and a direct report (acting director of nursing), but hey, I was open to anything, and it was a pleasant enough experience.

I then had the third with the general manager and the ICU director/chair of the medical advisory committee, an intensivist. I had figured it had better be the best job in the world after all that but sadly, it never really was—the bar had been set very high by North Shore Private and SATH, at least in their early days.

Sunnybank was a Healthscope hospital, and I had finally ended up employed by them with the hope that the reputation they had decades ago was no longer the truth. SATH chief executive officer provided an appropriate reference and one of the VMOs who had strongly disagreed with what had occurred with me, provided a second reference check.

I was offered the position and had to accept a $40k salary drop—oh yeah—that was a shocker. I did appreciate that I had been on a significant salary at SATH because I had incremented every year for 12 years; however, I had expected that at least some acknowledgement of that experience would be made.

Not so! But it was in Brisbane, and we had decided that we could cope with moving that far, so I accepted the position when offered. I was promised an annual bonus by my appointing general manager that would help bring up my salary, which disappeared during Covid, so that was that.

My new general manager was a breath of fresh air to work with after SATH chief executive officer simply because he was not a micro manager and essentially, just left me to get on with managing nursing matters and staff.

He managed VMO matters, as should occur in any acute private hospital. I soon discovered that Healthscope micromanaged every hospital executive to within an inch of their life and was probably not that surprised to discover that the chief executive officer I had briefly experienced at Prince of Wales Private all those years ago was now a senior manager at Healthscope as Qld state manager—I am fairly certain he did not remember me from Prince of Wales Private and I sure as hell did not remind him.

It seemed the ensuing years had softened his edges and he seemed a different man and leader than the one I had known. I thought I had certainly changed during the previous 19 years, so why not him.

I started in September 2019, a delayed start after my appointment in July, following a fabulous three-week holiday in Singapore, Sri Lanka and the Maldives, and happily settled into my director of nursing role, getting my head around being back within a private hospital group—Healthscope had hospitals all around Australia.

It was a bit of a shock to the system after 12+ years of freedom with just a board to report to but in a lot of ways was great—it was so nice to be back with a head office full of skilled experienced healthcare people.

To have lawyers and HR experts available or excellent risk managers or pretty much whatever you needed. So very nice after the lack of healthcare knowledge sometimes demonstrated from the SATH board.

Sunnybank introduced me to yet another non-surgical specialty that I had never before experienced, with it having not only a medical ward but also a rehab service. At Sunnybank, I learnt that not only are theatre and ICU staff special, but so are physiotherapists who have a real hang-up about not being treated the same as nurses.

Again, luck was on my side with an appropriately qualified rehab manager in place along with a great rehab physician.

In my first months at Sunnybank, I was not sure whether to be astounded or amused when I found out that the CCTV cameras that were in place throughout the hospital were installed after the general manager had his car tyres slashed. I had never heard of such a thing happening but would later discover that this happened to general manager's tyres more often than one might expect, at least in Brisbane!

Mind you, having those CCTV cameras came in handy on more than one occasion, helping us catch a VMO stealing N95 masks during the early days of Covid, and a nurse pilfering a narcotic drug from the recovery ward, with the latter appearing to look right at the camera, either not realising what it was or simply just not seeing it for what it was because she had become used to it.

Both made calling someone on their behaviour easy when you could produce a still photo from the CCTV footage which absolutely showed their guilt.

All was well with the world, if you exclude the Covid pandemic, until the general manager up and resigned in May 2020. He would not say where he was going but I knew in my bones that he was going to be the new chief executive officer at SATH—the role had been advertised recently, noting that my old boss was finally retiring.

His attraction to the role was probably helped in no small part by me sharing anecdotes about how great the hospital was. I still thought it was this even after everything.

The general manager had a background that included working for a health fund and I knew this would have been so attractive to the board at SATH because of the struggles the hospital had negotiating with health funds as a stand-alone facility with none of the power of a large group.

He merrily went off on gardening leave where he basically worked out his three months' notice from home and I got to act as the general manager and director of nursing for the next few months.

It was a great opportunity and I got to participate in the service planning for the hospital along with all of the other group general managers, supported by the latest Qld state manager, with my old Prince of Wales Private chief executive officer now in a much more senior role as chief operating officer (COO).

I worked my butt off and actually thought I was doing ok, but the reality was that I was not a Healthscope long-timer and Sunnybank was seen as a bit of a problem child that needed an experienced general manager.

It was sadly the feeling of staff that Sunnybank was the poor relative of all the other Healthscope hospitals and that we were treated accordingly. I can't say I saw much during my time there to negate this.

Around this time (June/July 2020), I started experiencing rectal bleeding, but I convinced myself that it was a haemorrhoid. I had only had a CT in February 2020 as part of my routine follow-up with my gynae oncologist, which was clear, so, I did not think it could be anything else.

Because I was so busy being the acting general manager/director of nursing, I did not see anyone about it straight away.

When Healthscope finally appointed the general manager from Brisbane Private Hospital as the acting general manager for Sunnybank as well as Brisbane Private, I was finally able to draw breath. Between acting as the general manager and all the dramas of Covid, the year had flown.

I had only met this new general manager briefly at the Healthscope manager's conference in early 2020, which my previous general manager managed to miss out on due to his health, and unfortunately, we had clashed over an employee.

We had appointed a new CSSD manager at Sunnybank who was previously at Brisbane Private, and this general manager refused to release her though she was complaining of being bullied.

Head office HR was involved, and it was a bit messy—my old general manager had made me deal with Brisbane Private general manager because it was about a clinical staff member even though technically, he probably should have.

I know—the story of my life. So, when she was appointed as my new general manager, you could say I was worried and wary.

I actually really liked her work style, which was more like my old SATH chief executive officer's style with more of a micro-managing focus, but she seemed to call a spade a spade, which had always been a trait that appealed to me.

I was then flat out as she converted everything that had been in place at Sunnybank to what she had at Brisbane Private Hospital, whether it was broken or not—no small job when it included everything from committee structures to VMO craft group meetings and so on.

In amongst this, I finally got a referral to a colorectal surgeon for a colonoscopy to address my haemorrhoid issue. I asked my gynae oncologist who I should see, so maybe some sixth sense was telling me that it should be someone he knew.

I finally had a colonoscopy in early August 2020, and they were unable to pass the colonoscope due to the recurrence of my ovarian cancer. That day, my hubby and I were devastated and it seemed almost like that first experience of being diagnosed all over again.

You know the drill—where is it, how bad is it?—how long have I got to live?—all on repeat again! We both cried as we tried to deal with it all again.

CT and MRI demonstrated that I needed a laparotomy, debulking (again) and anterior resection of the involved bowel. How lucky was I that it had perforated my bowel and caused the bleeding that flagged its existence—I never thought I would see the day I was grateful for cancer in my bowel and yet, here I was, very grateful.

What really sucked was that I had to finally tell Healthscope and Sunnybank executive, as well as the staff about my ovarian cancer history and this new challenge. I had really loved being somewhere where no-one knew my history and so, never treated me differently because of it.

But it was what it was, and I needed to just get on with it. Healthscope, and in particular, my old Prince of Wales Private chief executive officer were amazing and supported me incredibly throughout the process, allowing me to have sick leave in advance as well as organising for a nurse unit manager from Gold Coast Private to relieve me for the month I needed to be off work. Hmm—perhaps I should have worried about this!

My PET CT showed that again, they appeared to have got it all, so my uncanny luck with ovarian cancer continued. I had the month off and then returned to work where I continued to need to have weekly chemotherapy treatment.

Unlike my first experience where I could be treated where I worked at SATH, my oncology care was all at the Wesley still under the lovely oncologist who had taken over my care in Toowoomba—he now only worked in Brisbane.

I would have chemo from 7 on the Monday morning, then drive to work by lunchtime and stay until late afternoon after we had completed our weekly management teleconference with the state manager.

These phone calls considered KPIs and all things hospital performance and were some of that micro-managing I mentioned earlier. All simply my opinion!

A moment that has stayed with me from Sunnybank was a conversation I had with one of our neurosurgeons soon after my return to work and my disclosure about my ovarian cancer.

He presented to my office and proceeded to tell me that he could tell me something that would make me feel better—and he then proceeded to tell me that as bad as ovarian cancer is with its 85% recurrence rate, he could pip me at the post with his glioblastoma, a brain tumour with a 100% recurrence rate.

I was so shocked by his comment that I honestly responded with a choked laugh and said, "God, I am so sorry, but you are so right; you have made me feel better." I am unclear of his current status but remain always grateful for his generous visit and words.

Of course, this time around, I was now 58 and exhausted—still flat out keeping up with all the changes the acting general manager wanted me to make. Because she was general manager for Brisbane Private and Sunnybank, she mostly only spent two days a week with us, which meant that, like it or not, I got dragged back into dealing with VMO matters.

Yet again, I was tasked with having some unpleasant conversations with certain VMOs, which I should never have had to deal with but unfortunately, I did not feel that I could say no to her. She was feisty and scary, and coincidentally or not, she was short.

I managed to work through to February 2021, drawing the short straw to work over Christmas—another Healthscope action unlike every other private health group I had ever worked at that let executive and most department heads have the break they needed over Christmas while the hospital was managed by after-hours managers at a time when the hospital was usually nearly empty.

I had chemo the Monday before Christmas and I must admit that due to this last lot of chemo actually making me feel a bit sick, this Christmas Day was possibly worse than the one in 2015.

My first year at Sunnybank, my initial general manager was happy to let us implement the same Christmas fun I had experienced at SATH with a Christmas decoration competition throughout the hospital, even agreeing for he and I to dress up as Mr and Mrs Claus at our executive suite staff's insistence as part of our own department theme.

They had never done anything like it at Sunnybank and it really was amazing to see the joy experienced by staff, VMOs and patients; they all loved it. The general manager, finance manager and I also proceeded to serve Christmas breakfast to night duty staff on our main staff Christmas party day, and then we served lunch for staff on-site for our full Christmas lunch. It was fabulous fun, and I cannot recall a single unhappy person throughout the silly season.

And then, this general manager left and the new general manager or GM McScrooge arrived. No more Christmas decoration fun allowed—it was deemed too childish, unprofessional and messy and the hospital was only allowed to put up hotel themed garlands throughout the hospital that looked more like wreaths than Christmas decorations. How to suck the joy out of Christmas!

During late 2020 and early 2021, there were simmering issues with staff from one of the wards that I had managed really poorly—I unfortunately attempted to address complaints of bullying by one of the clinical managers and I believe I may have too easily believed a version of what events had unfolded.

I think, throughout my career, hearing about bullying was like a red rag to a bull and it was like my Achilles heel, and I simply could not tolerate it. The fact that I had managed things so poorly, even with the general manager's advice, was not a proud moment.

This issue had overflowed to a key VMO too and although the nurse unit manager informed the general manager and I both about her feeling bullied by this particular VMO—said general manager smartly delegated it to me to meet with the VMO and essentially, performance manage him.

The general manager had only ever had negative things to say about this key VMO and appeared to be enjoying causing him issues. I tried to get her to do it as general manager, but she had to go back to Brisbane Private or something similar. No surprises how that went.

I was so unhappy by this stage that I was looking for other jobs and had figured that it would only be a matter of time before the general manager got rid of me, particularly based on the tasks she was getting me to do, which were only making more people unhappy, because we simply did not click.

I was actually looking forward to it because as much as I was still trying my hardest to do my job, I was becoming more and more exhausted. I had really wanted to work until I was at least 60 but by this stage, I had my doubts that would be happening.

So, in early February 2021, when the general manager and the state manager called me into a meeting, it was no surprise to me that I was having my exit managed. They never really did tell me what I had apparently done but by that stage, I honestly did not care.

I believe lack of preparedness for ACHS review could have been mentioned but I was not sure what more I could have done when we had been visited multiple times by the head office quality team and I had been informed we were perfectly prepared.

I knew Brisbane Private had not long had a shocker of a review and yet their director of nursing survived unscathed—

he did have that something that I still didn't, no doubt. He was a he!

In any case, it was a huge, magnificent relief! Due to the fact that poor old Sunnybank had had so many executive managers sacked over the years, including mine and my original general manager's predecessors, we all agreed that announcing I had been terminated would go over a treat.

It was my suggestion that we announce I had resigned/retired due to my health—I knew that this would be a much better outcome for staff and VMOs if they believed this. Why am I telling the truth now? Because it is my truth to tell, and I am entitled to finally own it.

I am relatively certain that more than one staff member or VMO twigged that I had really been bumped, and possibly more than one of them was glad about it. If my leaving made people feel better, then I am glad, because my God, I was glad to go.

It was actually a really simple decision for me to decide to really retire. My hubby had been retired due to his health since that bowel obstruction issue in December 2016 and I had wanted to work until I was 60 but I really was just exhausted.

For the first time in my career, I could not wait to never go back! What almost made me laugh or choke, one or the other, was the general manager's parting comment, "If you haven't been sacked at least twice from an executive job in the private sector, then you haven't really worked," or something like that!

So, sack me once, shame on you; sack me twice, shame on me; sack me thrice; well bugger! Or as I would prefer to think 'third times a charm'. So, you director of nursing and director of clinical services out there with a sacking in your history, hold your head up—because frankly, if you have never been sacked at least once, then I suspect you can't be doing your job properly.

What were my takeaways from Sunnybank Private? That staff are fantastic and challenging and amazing wherever you are and just because other people write you off as not so great, it does not mean that you are not the best and Sunnybank staff, you are some of the best.

That there are nice and nasty doctors no matter where you are—your challenge is how you interact with them. And of course, last but not least that Healthscope was worth the wait—being part of the group was so rewarding and I loved being on the director of nursing clinical governance committee and chairing the Healthscope theatre management group.

Just like anywhere, there was great friendships and challenging ones—all worth it! Sadly, news I have received since my leaving Sunnybank is that the executive team merry-go-round continues with both DON and GM roles changing at least once, if not more.

Not a great way to build a solid care foundation with the culture you need to drive from the top down if no-one gets to stay long enough to achieve those things!

As for my original general manager—yes indeed, he did go and become the new chief executive officer at SATH much as I expected, starting in August 2021. We caught up for lunch soon after his commencement and addressed the elephant in the room—my history at SATH.

He told me in no uncertain terms that I should talk to a HR lawyer because I had a strong case for being constructively dismissed—a constructive dismissal is where essentially, you are forced to resign and that certainly did happen to me.

Sadly, for me, you can only contact Fair Work Australia about this occurring within three months of your termination/resignation and well over twelve months had passed since my adventure.

Plus, to be honest, I did not have the stomach for it. He also suggested to me that he had known about what had occurred with me at SATH before he had ever appointed me as the director of nursing at Sunnybank because he had talked to someone he knew in Toowoomba when he was recruiting me.

Whoever he spoke to had apparently been sympathetic about what had occurred to me. It was comforting to believe he had recruited me regardless, though I still doubted this feedback—I could not believe that he, or any other chief executive officer or general manager would have ignored the fact I was forced to resign due to a breakdown of a relationship with a doctor. At the end of the day, they are still a private hospital's bread and butter.

An update on the entire EMR/director of finance debacle at SATH was that it was well underway with much opposition from VMOs in my final months at SATH and I must admit it was something that I absolutely did not miss after I left.

It came as no surprise to me that soon after my Sunnybank general manager took over as chief executive officer at SATH that the director of finance was removed from his role and the hospital managed to disengage itself from the EMR contract, probably at some cost.

I am afraid this was not an item that received a positive picture from me when talking about my years at SATH, although I have little doubt that the entire mess was probably laid at my feet after I was gone.

This regularly occurred with any sacked executive managers that I followed into a role—everything wrong in the place was apparently suddenly their fault. I am sure the original SATH chief executive officer regrets ever listening to the director of finance about the EMR now, with the latter no doubt contributing to the hospital's apparent ongoing decline.

Following my leaving Sunnybank Private, I guess the question may also be asked about why I never went to Fair Work about an unfair dismissal claim for any of my dismissals. And yes, even though I thought they were all unfair, it does not mean any of them would have been deemed to be so.

The sad reality was that if you earned more than $138,900, which even on my reduced Sunnybank salary I still exceeded, you were not eligible to apply for it. Currently, the cap is $162,000 (from 2022).

If a successful claim is made, the maximum payment is 26 weeks or 6 months' pay, which supports why the major health groups such as Ramsay Health and Healthscope both usually pay this amount when they terminate you from an executive manager role.

So essentially, unfair dismissal probably does not apply to any executive manager on a reasonable salary, or any other worker earning in excess of this in Australia.

Since finishing work in February 2021, I managed to finish chemo that time around in May 2021—unfortunately, the immunotherapy drug, Avastin, I had been having three weekly caused me to develop malignant hypertension (acute high blood pressure) and I ended up admitted to the Wesley under a cardiologist for a week.

After incrementing anti-hypertensives for the week, I was finally discharged on the maximum I could take necessitating a Webster pack. Sad but true! I was then in relative remission until late 2021 when I was restarted on chemo after early signs of recurrence.

All of these times, I had been having Carboplatin as one of my chemo drugs—the main ovarian cancer chemo drug of choice and unfortunately, in May 2022, it became apparent that I had become platinum resistant, and this drug no longer worked.

My oncologist, who had been the oncologist I moved to in Toowoomba after the mess with my original oncologist, then had the difficult task of telling me that potentially with my cancer left untreated, I had 6-12 months to live. Confronting MUCH!

But he also offered to refer me over to his colleague at Icon at Mater Private South Brisbane to see if I might qualify for one of the clinical trials he coordinated. With nothing to lose, I, of course, said yes.

Then, I had the fortune to come into the care of my current brilliant medical oncologist. He is a British trained oncologist with a special interest and experience with ovarian cancer and coordinates a number of clinical trials in Australia as both the Australian lead and international lead.

I am ecstatic to be in his care and far more optimistic for my future—and hopeful that I will have a bit of one. After meeting him in June 2022, I was screened for the clinical trial drug AK112 inclusion, which included CTs and blood tests and a biopsy of a tumour in my groin that was easily accessible for needle biopsy.

AK112 was an immunotherapy trial drug and was being used in multiple types of cancer treatment. Part of the criteria for inclusion in the trial included that you had to have exhausted all usual treatment options—Carboplatin no longer worked for me, must have metastatic disease—it was spreading to my lymph system, and have a tumour large enough to measure—I had one in my groin according to CT.

This latter allowed measurement and monitoring at future CT scans to determine if the drug is working. What I surmised from all of the criteria was that basically, you need to be dying, but not be too sick!

It also brought home the fact that cancer patients can't just put their hand up for an immunotherapy clinical trial drug—there are very specific criteria you need to meet. And I was grateful to my Wesley oncologist for getting me to where I was—his difficult task telling me of my potential shortened lifespan enabled me to claim my life insurance and tidy up other aspects of my life.

After retiring in February 2021, I became interested in the fight for the voluntary assisted dying (VAD) legislation in Queensland. This legislation was designed to implement a legal process where persons who were suffering and dying would have the opportunity to request medical assistance to end their life.

I was well aware from my many years in nursing leadership, particularly those at SATH where we had a palliative care service, that the current process kind of did the job but was in no way pleasant or legal.

Patients at end of life who no longer wished to suffer or prolong their life would be commenced on a syringe driver containing a cocktail of drugs such as morphine and over a period of days would deteriorate and die.

I saw the process with my own mother, so I was well acquainted with it and I had no wish to experience it myself if I had a choice.

Through local contacts, I ended up involved with the Go Gentle group headed up by Andrew Denton. His work in this area throughout Australia is ground-breaking and our subsequent success in Qld and other states was in no small part due to his commitment to the cause.

I was approached at one stage in 2021 by Go Gentle to provide an interview outlining my cancer background and my thoughts about current palliative care. I agreed to written media and had a submission about my health and palliative care thoughts included in the information pack that went to Qld MPs prior to their vote on the legislation.

An initial request to be more of a face for the story was made; however, I declined, stating that I did not want any healthcare haters to come out swinging for me because I dared to posit the reality of what our current palliative care service entailed. At that stage, I really did not wish to paint such a target on myself.

I was as thrilled as all other VAD campaigners when the voluntary assisted dying act 2021 was passed in Qld parliament on 16 September 2021, coming into effect January 2023.

It gave me a great sense of relief to know that when my time comes, I will hopefully have the option to go 'gently into that sweet good night'.

I have a friend who is a certified VAD practitioner with Qld health who has assured me she will help me with whatever assistance I need sorting out my access to VAD when the time comes, and this eases my mind no end—I will have to think about whether I will really take advantage of her generosity and put her in such a shitty position.

Over the ensuing years, I have been on two trial immunotherapy drugs, with the initial one AK-112 triggering my malignant hypertension, and the latter AMT-151 just not really working.

My ovarian cancer has reduced to be almost clear of my lymph system following treatment with Paclitaxol (yes, I lost my hair again; always a fun thing to have happen but again managed with an awesome wig) before reappearing throughout my lymph system.

I had been re-challenged with Carboplatin, that ovarian cancer chemo drug I became resistant to in early 2022, as well as a new one, Gemcitabine, and my PET CT in January 2024 had shown a reduction in my current cancer.

My treatments of chemo were interspersed with my needing units of blood because unfortunately, both drugs really knocked my bone marrow about. The sad reality is that chemo does not just kill the bad shit, it wrecks much more of you than that and so, you cannot just keep having it forever without breaks.

I had a repeat PET CT in March 2024, which unfortunately showed that my nasty was on the march again; dare I say, cha cha cha! Two steps forward and one step back!

After seeing my oncologist in early April 2024, we agreed for me to remain off treatment for four weeks with a hope that I will then make it onto an immunotherapy trial—you need to have been treatment free for four weeks before any of the trials.

That was dependent on me remaining relatively asymptomatic—which unfortunately I did not manage, experiencing vaginal bleeding after about two weeks. A stint in hospital confirmed that my pelvic tumour was trying very hard to be a nuisance and had started to breach my vagina.

The consideration of whether or not I would require a laparoscopic bowel bypass (with stoma) or repair of a potential rectovaginal fistula was very real and very terrifying.

Fortunately for me, neither have been required just yet though my lovely colorectal surgeon has assured me he is on the bench for when I need him (which I likely will). My hospitalisation also identified that I had acute right hydronephrosis, where my tumour was pushing on my right ureter, causing urine to back up in my right kidney.

This was managed with the insertion of a right ureteric stent in late April 2024. And as per usual, none of these surgical options or actual procedures worried me at all—all thanks to my old theatre nurse belief in surgery and good outcomes. It never occurred to me that I would not be fine!

In May 2024, I was then lucky to start my third immunotherapy clinical trial of the two drugs—BGB-A3055 and BGB—A317. I am hopeful that these will turn out to be my 'third times a charm' immunotherapy treatment, which will finally offer me a cancer free future.

Of course, the feedback that the drugs have had a good result but I absolutely will have a side effect of some type— an itis of some type (inflammation such as myocarditis, pneumonitis, hepatitis, etc.) was a bit confronting but hell, what is a little itis between friends?

Within two weeks of my initial treatment, I promptly came down with colitis, the most common side effect apparently. Presenting to the emergency department with a temperature of 39.5 and increasing gastroenteritis certainly demonstrated to me that you can feel really crap and still survive.

I then proceeded to have a week in hospital at the Mater South Brisbane in ward 8 north. I had a chance to enjoy the pleasure of some excellent nursing care and loved being able to talk to the nurses, particularly some of the students who were absolute stars.

I have always held nursing in the highest regard and the chance that I might in some small way shape their thinking as a possible future nurse leader remained very rewarding. (Although I imagine my steroid mania from the 1.5g IV steroid I was commenced on may have presented me as the crazy old DON in room 843. ☺)

The entire ward staff are amazing, working their butts off having to deal with nurse: patient ratios, a sad nurses union and public health push.

Hearing they have a 1 nurse to 10 patients ratio on a night shift in such a high acuity ward was truly concerning because no 10 patients are the same and I will always preach that you should staff to patient acuity (how sick they are) and staff safety and not blind stupid numbers!

The patient I was on day 2 suffering rigors from a high temperature with multiple IV drugs required to help me recover was a very different picture to the patient I presented at day 7 when I was back to normal and fully independent, requiring little care.

After discharge, I now have the fun task of weaning off the steroid and the uncertainty of waiting to see if I will have another go at the BGB cherry; but that is ok, because if not, my amazing oncologist may yet pull another rabbit out of his hat!

When off trial drugs, I am monitored 3 monthly with a PET CT to determine how my cancer is travelling—though during any trial drug treatments, you are only reviewed with CTs which do not show the same detail—they simply want to measure the size change in tumours to determine the success of the trial drug.

Until such time as you have ever personally experienced a PET CT to identify if, and how far, your cancer has spread, it is difficult to describe the associated terror. Oncology staff certainly understand the term *scanxiety* really well, with one of mine telling me that they actually experience it on our behalf too—probably why burnout is a real risk in oncology wards!

I generally spend the entire time in the PET CT machine chanting, "Please don't light up, please don't light up"—that is kind of what a PET CT does—it lights up with all different colours—with the different colours demonstrating physiological changes and cellular activity.

You start a sugar free diet the day before and then have IV fluid containing radioactive tracer attached to dextrose in the hour before your scan. Cancer loves sugar and it attracts the sugar with the tracers and subsequently lights up.

In the year or so after retirement, before I decided to start writing this memoir, I did a couple of painting classes at the

Brisbane Institute of Art—I had loved art at school and had an urge to get back into it though I did not know where to start.

Completing 'Painting for beginners' and a couple of other classes was well worth it, allowing me to find a passion for using acrylic paints. I found my preference for the latter probably related to my lack of patience at the best of times.

Acrylic dries very quickly and you can effectively complete a painting in a day if you go for it, unlike oils and other mediums that take weeks and months to complete. I also further indulged my craft bone by completing a ring making class one weekend, which allowed me to make two gold rings; neither of these are quite the same as my sister's craft DNA where they sew and knit and do all of that other clever stuff that was never my cup of tea.

I also continued to ponder my bucket list. I had started one soon after my initial diagnosis in December 2015 and what I learnt over the years as I ticked items off is that you cannot have a finite bucket list of things you really want to do before you die—you need to keep adding to it.

It's a bit like always trying to have a holiday planned as something to look forward to. I have got to tick off most of my list with the main exclusion being 'eating lunch at a winery under the Tuscan sun', probably one that is on everyone's list.

Unfortunately for me, my oncologist does not want me going overseas anymore because of the very real risk of something nasty happening health wise occurring with me. I also can no longer access travel insurance, which is a bit of a bugger!

But that's ok because there is still a lot of this beautiful country (Australia) that I have not seen, so I might yet make it to some of those spots.

After most of my appointments, I continue to update my social media since it is the best way for me to keep my family and friends up to date without multiple calls and allows my truth to continue to be out there.

The feedback I receive really does help me to remain positive. Have I always been so optimistic—yes, mostly! But I am only human and I have had at least one moment thinking it was all too much.

It was the day I was discharged from hospital after having my second lot of major abdominal surgery in August 2020 and I had managed to climb the two flights of stairs in our three-storey townhouse.

My wound was sore, in fact, everything was sore and I just had a moment of complete self-pity and being miserable when I told my hubby that I hoped that it was the last big fight I needed to have because I did not think I could do it again.

And hubby, God love him, hugged me and told me very firmly, "Yes you will keep fighting and you will do whatever you need to do."

I had another shake it off Tay Tay moment much like that first Christmas and agreed that of course I would. The moments of living in your personal grief and regretting the things you will one day miss are ok to have, you just need to remember not to dwell in them. Dwelling sucks the life out of everything! You need to remember the joy to be found with the little things!

I remain endlessly optimistic, helped in no small part by the excellent team of oncology staff from Icon South Brisbane and my fabulous oncologist. The oncology nurses and other amazing oncology support staff in the day chemo section who do their best to keep us upbeat and hopeful are absolute stars!

Of course, my husband Phillip, my family and our friends are also a constant source of positive energy for me. I made it clear in the beginning with my family that as much as I appreciate their tears for me, I have no desire to witness them, they can save them until I am gone!

Harsh but necessary to maintaining a positive mind-set. I hope to have a chance to plan my own funeral and even write my own eulogy—I would like to copy my cousin Chris who had a 'Celebration of his life' instead of a funeral when he left us in May 2024.

The other thing that plays on my mind is how I can help support Phillip when I am gone—it is easy to get so wrapped up in your own potential future demise that you forget the terror of being the one left behind, especially when you are part of a childless couple as we have been for so many years.

I can only leave him in the care of our friends and family and remind them all that while ever they talk about and remember me, I am still here. And at the end of the day, I may not even go first. No-one's future is promised and we all need to remember that!

Although I had retired in February 2021, I decided to renew my nurses registration in May 2021 because it just seemed too hard to let something that had been such a big part of my life go.

However, by May 2022, I had come to terms with the fact that there really was no point in me maintaining my registration since between my need for regular treatment, my deafness (an earlier gift from Carboplatin) and increasing brain fog due to age, menopause and chemo, I was no longer competent to be a Registered Nurse.

I still feel a little like I had severed a limb when I let it go but as is the case with so many things in life, all good things do eventually need to come to an end.

For all of this, I am actually thankful for what occurred at SATH, the best and worst moments of my career—the reality is that if what occurred up there had not happened, I would not have found my way to Brisbane and ultimately to the care of the oncologist I am now with. I am sure that my outcomes may have been very different had my life not played out as it has.

I have long come to terms with the fact that I am now a chronic ovarian cancer sufferer and I will be doing the long dance with it in one form or another until she totally trips me up.

I like to think of it as a cha cha cha, as mentioned briefly previously, because I definitely seem to take 2 steps forward and then at least one step back. As much as I have no way of knowing what lays ahead for me, I have a pretty good idea and I have no delusions about how things will play out for me. Sometimes being a nurse sucks and ignorance would be bliss. But it has all been so worth it.

If this story actually makes it to publication, I hope I am around to see it but if not—that's ok—I had a great life, including a great career.

My legacy may not be my own children, but I will include that it was some of the excellent clinical managers I got to work with, and maybe had a little influence on over the years—my theatre management team at Westmead Private, a couple of the ward managers at North Shore Private, Jeff, at so many of my roles including Prince of Wales Private, Westmead, SATH and Sunnybank—yes, I kept stealing him, and far from least, Katie and Liv at SATH! Thank you for the memories, peeps—you guys all rock!

Quick summary of takeaways:

1. You cannot hide what you are. Staff and colleagues will always show their true colours if you give them enough time.
2. Do not pop your head up where men with power will see you—do not be a right fighter! (Yeah, you do still need to do the right thing though.)
3. You shape yourself to your environment, you do not expect them to change shape for you—you are the implant.
4. Once you have stepped up to a more senior role, it is hard to go back to being a plebe.
5. No-one is irreplaceable, no matter how fabulous they are.
6. You should never go back—no matter who asks you.
7. It is often not what you know but who you know.
8. Sometimes, you should do the right thing even if it is not considered the correct thing to do.
9. Your team can make you, or any other manager for that matter, look really good—you just have to respect them and let them do their jobs. Let people do what they do well!
10. Don't believe your own press!
11. Spread the fairy dust—go out and around the hospital and be seen by staff. Say hello and talk to them—don't just hide in your office.

12. If it ain't broke, don't try to fix it!
13. A DCS/DON must always have an excellent relationship with your CEO, this is usually made easier if they were the one to appoint you, because if there is ever trouble at the top of a private hospital, you are usually the one that will be chopped.
14. If you do not have a backup plan for your role—stop being so arrogant and succession train someone. You are not irreplaceable, so get over yourself.
15. As the DCS/DON, always stay the hell away from doctor matters—they are not for you, DCS or DON. Leave that crap to the CEO/GM whether he/she has the balls for it or not. NOT YOUR JOB! Unless you are protecting a nurse, leave them to it!
16. Try to be a consultative manager and let your direct reports have a voice. Give credit where it is due—NEVER take credit for someone else's work—that is grotesque and lacking in integrity.
17. What has been seen cannot be unseen—once a staff member brings an issue to you, then you need to deal with it. There is a great cat meme to go with this that graced the wall of many of my offices.
18. You DONs and DCSs out there with a sacking in your history, hold your head up—because frankly, if you have never been sacked at least once, then I suspect you can't be doing your job properly. 😊
19. Do not ever forget that no matter how friendly you get with that doctor, that if it comes down to you or them, they will always pick them! Just human nature!

20. There are great staff and crappy staff everywhere, and there are great VMOs and crappy ones everywhere. I hope you find only the former of each.
21. And last but far from least—just because the big C comes for you, it does not mean that life is immediately over. Laugh lots, dream big and remember to stop and smell the roses.